werewolf vs vampire

blood|rivals

Taylor Lautner
The Biography

werewolf vs vampire

blood|rivals

Taylor Lautner
The Biography

JOHN BLAKE

Published by John Blake Publishing Ltd,
3 Bramber Court, 2 Bramber Road,
London W14 9PB, England

www.johnblakepublishing.co.uk

First published in paperback in 2009

ISBN: 978 1 84454 916 0

British Library Cataloguing-in-Publication Data:

A catalogue record for this book is available from the British Library.

Design by www.envydesign.co.uk

Printed in Great Britain by CPI Bookmarque, Croydon, CR0 4TD

1 3 5 7 9 10 8 6 4 2

Papers used by John Blake Publishing are natural, recyclable products made
from wood grown in sustainable forests. The manufacturing processes
conform to the environmental regulations of the country of origin.

To Nia, for all her help and support

Martin Howden's work has appeared in several newspapers and magazines through his job as a showbiz editor for World Entertainment News Network. He currently writes for Yahoo! Movies as a freelance film journalist. He is also the author of *Lily Allen – Living Dangerously* and *Danny Dyer – The Real Deal*.

Contents

Introduction

The Twilight Saga is the classic tale of a love triangle that has divided the nation. Who should Bella Swan choose? The dashing, mysterious and undead Edward Cullen? Or the loyal, besotted and shapeshifting Jacob Black? The endless debate for *Twilight* fans rages on.

But now, it's more than that. The rivals are no longer confined to the pages of a book, but have exploded onto the scene as two of the biggest upcoming Hollywood stars of the moment: Robert Pattinson and Taylor Lautner. For millions of fans around the world, Taylor Lautner *is* Jacob Black. And for them, there is only one side: Team Jacob.

Since you've flicked onto the Taylor Lautner side, you're obviously a big fan of the young actor with a big smile and an even bigger heart. And you'll be pleased to hear that Taylor's portrayal of the down-to-earth Jacob with a dangerous werewolf side isn't that far off his off-camera personality as well – he's proven to everyone that he has the fighting spirit to really sink his teeth into the role.

Taylor may look like butter wouldn't melt in his mouth, but don't be fooled – Team Jacob has got a fighting chance with Taylor leading the charge.

Welcome to his story.

chapter one
The Karate Kid

'From karate, I had the confidence and drive to push myself.' – Taylor Lautner

Taylor Daniel Lautner was born on 11 February 1992 to the joy of his parents Deborah and Daniel, a software manager and airline pilot respectively. It would be a long time before their son would land the role of Jacob Black in the *Twilight* series, but even as a child Taylor seemed destined to play a werewolf. 'I don't remember it, but my parents tell me I'd bite other kids. I was a biter at day care!' he told *Grand Rapids Press*.

Born in the west Michigan town of Grand Rapids, he lived in a little house on Rosewood Avenue. Because both parents' relatives lived nearby, Taylor was never short of affection, and the young boy was rarely slow to flash his cute smile to charming effect. He even wowed staff at the hospital when he was born!

He had an incredibly happy childhood, and he still misses his home town, especially the local Hudsonville ice cream. He also misses the 'green, the lakes and the changing seasons'. We bet he doesn't miss the cold though; Grand Rapids is one of the snowiest cities in the US, with an average of 72 inches of snow each year.

Talking about his home town to *Grand Rapids Press*, he said, 'I love coming back here. In LA, whatever you do for fun, you gotta spend money. Here, you go jet-skiing on a lake. It's such a fun place for me. I go fishing with one set of grandparents, I go quad bike riding with the other set. We go trap shooting. It's so much fun. Here, people are way more down to earth.'

When he was six, Taylor became a big brother to Makena. Just as Taylor was spoilt for affection, so was Makena. Taylor was about as good a big brother as a baby sister could want. 'My sister and I would always be spies when I was younger. We'd be in the house and I'd hide something, and I'd act like we were secret agents and spies. I'd tell her that it was really happening, and she still believes me to this day.'

By the time Makena was born, the family had moved to a bigger home. And the reason they moved was because the family had a terrifyingly lucky escape. Taylor was four at the time and his dad was away once more on a flight. His mother

2

decided that the two of them should visit one of his aunts and stay the night there. That very night, their house burned down.

Taylor looks back at the incident now and reflects just how lucky he is. 'The police called and told us our house had burned down. If my aunt hadn't invited us to sleep over... Well, wow!'

Taylor seems to take up hobbies and interests like a sponge. He is a complete sports nut and the sight of a young Taylor wrestling with his friends in and out of the house, no matter the weather, was a regular one. And if he wasn't wrestling, then he would be playing a number of other sports that took his interest, including swimming, baseball, soccer, horse riding and basketball.

One of Taylor's big loves was American football, which he was very good at, making the high school team. 'I played football my whole life and had to give it up last year because I had to miss too many practices,' he said recently. 'It was kind of rough for me. It is kind of hard watching the high school football team now. I played running back and slot receiver, and strong safety on defence.

'I love sports,' he added. 'If I could, I'd be on a team. If there's an excuse to play football, I'm there.'

It wasn't just sport that Taylor took a fancy to. He was also fascinated by acting and quickly dreamt of becoming an actor. But when Taylor was six, he discovered something else that would take over his young life. He enrolled at nearby Fabiano's Karate & Fitness Center, and he took to martial arts incredibly well.

The karate school owner, Tom Fabiano, remembered Taylor as a willing, hardworking and talented pupil. 'A lot of boys that age are bouncing off the walls, but Taylor was always deliberate, focused. He wasn't a typical kid. He always worked extra hard.'

Recalling his karate lessons at school, Taylor told *karateangels.com*, 'A friend of mine through my mom's work had his sons in karate and my parents took me to check out the class. I liked it and began karate when I was six. I really liked class because of all the games we got to play, like swords and spears, sensei says, etc. I didn't really care too much for the push-ups and all the hard work. I really started because of the fun games.'

It quickly became clear that Taylor was a natural, winning local contests with ease. At seven years old he shocked everyone when he competed in the nationals and won three trophies.

His skill at martial arts is even more impressive when you consider that Taylor didn't just want to be king of the mat, but also king of the big screen. Just like Bruce Lee, Chuck Norris and Steven Seagal before him, Taylor wanted to showcase his martial arts talents to a wider audience. Taylor's particular role model was Jean-Claude Van Damme. 'I'd love to be an action director or writer or be in action films, just like him,' he said.

Acting was something Taylor considered, but with martial arts taking up much of his life, where would he find the time to learn the craft? In a strange twist of fate, while competing at the national championship he met a new instructor who would not only teach him a new form of martial arts that he had invented, but also give him the guidance needed to break into the movie business.

The karate instructor was Mike Chat, who played Blue Lightspeed Ranger in the *Power Rangers* TV show and movie, which were hugely popular in the late 1990s. Chat was impressed with what he saw of Taylor and invited him to his Extreme Martial Arts (XMA) Camp in Los Angeles. For someone who was a fan of the show, it didn't take long for Taylor to say yes to being taught by one of his screen heroes!

XMA was a new form of martial arts invented by Thailand-born Chat, a seven-time world karate champion. It combines dance, yoga, tae kwon do and kickboxing to fun and entertaining effect.

For Taylor, who had only been taught in a traditional martial arts style, this was a huge chance – and it was something he immediately grasped. 'I fell in love. By the end of the camp, I was doing aerial cartwheels with no hands. My favourite martial artist is Mike Chat. He's helped me so much.'

Asked about the difference between extreme and

regular martial arts, Taylor explained, 'Regular martial arts is traditional, with no music and no flips choreographed into it. But extreme martial arts is choreographed to music. It's very fast-beat up-tempo and you put a lot of acrobatic manoeuvres into the routine.

'[My favourite move is] called a corkscrew. It's a back flip off one leg and then you do a 360 [degree turn] in the air and I land it in the splits. I was the first competitor to ever land that in the national karate circuit.'

Taylor decided to keep up with both his traditional karate classes and XMA lessons with Chat. The former saw him landing a black belt at eight, but the latter was a little more difficult. With Chat's classes in LA and with Taylor's dad often away because of his job as a pilot, a regular commute from Michigan to LA could have proved problematic.

But Taylor's parents and Chat worked out a training schedule that would see him flying to LA as often as he could, sometimes even taking an overnight flight back to Grand Rapids to make sure he didn't miss out on an important test at school.

They did this for a year and it was obvious to everyone involved that Taylor was something of a star. At eight he won three gold medals and became the Junior World Forms and Weapons Champion at the World Karate Association Championship. At nine he followed that with the Warrior Trophy Cup for the entire Under 17 age group at a World Karate Association competition.

You might think that while Taylor was causing a splash in the martial arts world his education would be suffering. Not so. 'I get mostly As with an occasional A- here and there,' said Taylor. 'The key is an open communication with my teacher. My parents and me are in close communication with my teachers to make sure I'm not missing anything and understanding assignments. This doesn't mean it's not been difficult, because it has. I think once the school understands that my education is important to me, then they are understanding. The last week has been really tough. I've had to stay up till 10.30 or 11.00 pm each night to make sure all my homework is done.'

Eventually, however, the demanding schedule began to take its toll and Taylor decided to take a year off from competing in karate tournaments. He would still train but, after three years of intense training, he needed a rest. The break also meant that he could go back to enjoying playing other sports, such as American football, and enjoy spending more time with his friends.

But Taylor missed the satisfaction of competing in martial arts tournaments, and in 2003 he rejoined the circuit. He quickly won the World Junior Weapons Championship and found himself ranked number one in the world at the North American

Sport Karate Association's Black Belt Open Forms, Musical Weapons, Traditional Weapons and Traditional Forms.

Because of the success of his acting career and the fact that karate training would take up most of his evenings and weekends, Taylor has had to give up competing. "I gave up karate for acting, and now I'm very glad I made that choice. Karate is just a horrible mix with acting. I had to pick either karate or acting, and I picked acting. But I still sometimes train at my house, just to keep up the skill.'

Taylor might have chosen acting, but just as with karate he would have to work extremely hard, learn his craft and make sacrifices. In fact, his whole family would have to.

chapter two

Taylor Makes his Mark

'I would love to do an extreme action movie and choreograph my own stunts.' – Taylor Lautner

Chat was not only hugely impressed with Taylor's martial arts ability but saw that the young charismatic kid could have a future in Hollywood too. 'He saw that I wasn't shy, that I was confident and that I talked a lot,' revealed Taylor. And Taylor wasn't going to say no to such an offer. He was desperate to get into acting.

'The first audition that my karate instructor sent me out on was a Burger King commercial,' Taylor told *Reel Answers*. 'It was kind of like a karate audition in that they were basically looking for martial arts stuff. And they were looking for someone older, but he wanted to send me anyway to get the experience.

'So I met with the casting director, we talked, and

she asked for some poses. It was funny though, because at the time, I didn't even know what a pose was [laughs]! I was only seven. But I learned quickly and did some poses for them. And I really liked it. I thought it went well but I didn't get it.'

Despite not landing the part, Taylor was well and truly bitten by the acting bug. So he was no doubt overjoyed when Chat asked him if he wanted to go to California for a month to try and land some movie and TV roles. A chance to be near Hollywood was too good an opportunity to turn down, but he still had doubts.

'At first, I wasn't interested,' he told *Teen Vogue*, 'but he said I could stay at his house for a few weeks, meet with some agents, go on auditions.' By the end of that month, Taylor says, 'I liked it. Taking on roles that were the opposite of what I could be in real life? That's still my favourite thing.'

Chat spoke warmly to *SportsMartialArts.com* about his passion for helping youngsters out. 'I've always liked helping people. I started teaching at an early age and I think the greatest pleasure I get out of the martial arts is giving back to the martial arts community. But it is more seeing kids develop and being able to play a part in the development of a person – that is what I find most rewarding.

'And the kids that I train, they are developing themselves as martial artists but more importantly as people and the skills that they are learning through their training, through their competing, and through their travelling they will have for life. And a lot of the kids are interested in doing entertainment work.

'Luckily, through the work I have done, I've been able to establish a pretty good network of relationships out in LA with agents and managers where I can provide opportunities for kids that maybe they would otherwise not have for a long time because I have been there and know the ins and outs.'

Asked in 2002 about his success stories, Chat said, 'John Stork, probably the least physically gifted but one of the hardest working with incredible potential out of any of my Team Chat kids. We worked very hard with him. First audition ever, he booked a national Burger King commercial where he played his dream character GoKu from *Dragon Ball Z*.

'Taylor Lautner, two months after signing with an agent, he booked a film called *Shadow Fury* which is actually just being released in Japan this month, and Taylor and John both played roles in it. Taylor was a martial arts fighting clone and John played an older version of the character. Taylor has done a lot of print work and other things like the Ultimate TV Microsoft commercial.'

Chat believed the reason for their success was down to their training. 'It's funny because when you go to LA there are over one million SAG [Screen Actors Guild] union actors and over one million extras. You look at the kids, and they say it is one in a million. You could be up against thousands and thousands of different kids. And because these kids have developed themselves and gained confidence and experience performing in front of other people, it is easy in front of a camera for them because they are so used to it.

'A lot of actors start out in the theatre or on stage and they are not used to being in a room full of people. You go to an audition and it is one casting director and then you go to a call-back and it's a producer, director, client and like, 20 people in the room. It can be kind of intimidating and I think that [performance in tournaments] is what has gotten these kids so far.'

Indeed, as soon as Taylor agreed to give acting a try, he got several auditions. It was a great vindication that he had made the right choice – especially as he booked his first role so soon after testing the waters in Hollywood. In 2001, he starred in martial arts action film *Shadow Fury*. It wasn't a big part but it was one that saw him fight on screen just like his hero Van Damme.

From the success of that, he was soon receiving offers from casting agents all over LA to come and read for parts. Once again Taylor found himself commuting from his home town to Hollywood. 'They'd call at nine or ten at night,' he said, 'which was six or seven their time, and say, "We've got an audition tomorrow – can you be there?" We'd leave really early in the morning and get there about noon. I'd get to the audition in the afternoon, take the red-eye back to Grand Rapids, then go to school.'

It was a crazy schedule, and one that couldn't last much longer. In the back of his mind, Taylor knew there could be very tough decisions to be made. Knowing there was no chance they could keep commuting every time he got an audition, he would have to convince his parents to move the family to Hollywood.

They decided to head to LA for a month, to see if it was worth making the move permanent. Despite attending several auditions, Taylor didn't land one part. It seemed his chance to conquer Hollywood was coming to an end, but on the day they were to head back to Michigan, Taylor received a call-back for a role. He wasn't successful in getting the part, but it showed his parents that he'd made enough of an impression to at least be considered.

His parents decided to extend their time in LA for six months, and Taylor did eventually land a role, as one of the voices in *The Rugrats Movie*. It was then that Taylor's family decided to move for good.

'It was a very, very hard decision,' Taylor concedes. 'Our family and friends did not want us to go. But our choices were: We could stay in Michigan and I could give up acting. I would have had to because it would have been crazy to continually fly out from Michigan to California each time there was an audition! Or we could move to California and I could continue to act. I told my parents I didn't want to give up acting. And after weighing the good with bad, they agreed to move.'

His parents had seen how hard Taylor had worked for this opportunity – the long commutes, the hours that could have been spent with his friends were instead being used up in casting agencies' waiting rooms – and they decided the sacrifice was worth it. Besides, they had brought him up in a responsible and grounded manner, so they had no fears that Hollywood would change their son.

'We kept him in public school as long as we could, so he could be with his peers,' Dan Lautner told *Grand Rapids Press*. 'We give him responsibilities at home – chores he has to do. He gets an allocated allowance and he has to budget it. We're trying to teach him things, so that when he goes out on his own, he'll be prepared.'

Taylor enrolled in Valencia High School in Santa Clarita, where he stayed before graduating early because of his film success. He went on to take college classes during filming. Despite having superb combat skills, Taylor insists that he never used them in school, preferring to keep away from any of the unruly classmates. 'Nobody's ever wanted to start a fight. I stay away from all that stuff. It's never really happened.'

After making his move to LA permanent, roles in *My Wife and Kids, The Bernie Mac Show* and *Summerland* followed. The first of these gave Taylor a chance to actually act out a complete different persona. 'I got to be a bully and push this little kid around! That was fun because I'm normally not a bully, because my parents wouldn't allow me to do that. I'm just not that person, but it was fun to experience something new.'

In 2005, Taylor – now 13 – began to enjoy some regular voice work. Not only were there roles in *What's New, Scooby-Doo?*, *The Adventures of Silas and Brittany* and *He's a Bully, Charlie Brown*, but he bagged a recurring role as the voice of Youngblood on the cartoon series *Danny Phantom*. It was a role that he had immense fun with.

'My favourite one so far was probably Youngblood on *Danny Phantom*. I've done three episodes so far and he's a lot of fun to voice. Probably because I'm a kid – bully – pirate. I'm an evil ghost and a pirate and get to say stuff like: "ARRRGH!"'

But it was live action that Taylor wanted to make an impact with, and he got his wish the same year when he landed a major role in *The Adventures of Sharkboy and Lavagirl* – the latest family film by *Spy Kids* director Robert Rodriguez.

Recalling how he got the part, Taylor said, 'Well, my agent got me the audition to meet with the casting director, and I just did my scenes that my agent faxed to me. About two weeks later, we found out that Robert Rodriguez and his son Racer [who came up with the idea for the film] wanted to meet with me at their hotel room in LA. So I went down and met with them and did my scenes for the casting director and Robert. And then Robert took out his own video camera and wanted to tape me. He asked for a superhero pose and I did one of my martial arts moves. I stand on one hand and I'm upside down and my legs are in a split position. And his son really liked that.'

But Taylor couldn't celebrate getting the part just yet. 'Unfortunately, LA was just the first spot that they stopped at before auditioning throughout the rest of the country,' he added. 'But fortunately, thousands of auditions later, they came back to me and told me I got the part.

'We went out to dinner to celebrate,' remembered Taylor. 'We went out with friends and I had a surprise at a restaurant with some friends. And we were all very excited when we found out. We couldn't sleep.'

Rodriguez said, 'He was the first actor we saw for *Sharkboy and Lavagirl* and we picked him right off. We knew he was the guy. He had so much personality. It's no surprise to me that he was going to go on to great things. He kind of made himself. In fact, he may have walked in fully formed.'

Taylor played Sharkboy, one half of a superhero team dreamed up by a ten-year-old boy who is constantly getting bullied at school. However, Max – the bullied boy – gets a shock when the figments of his imagination turn out not only to be real but also to need his help.

Talking about his character, Taylor said, 'Well, first of all, he's a superhero. When he was younger, about five years old, he was separated from his father in a storm. His father was a marine biologist and after his father disappeared, he was all alone... except for the sharks.

'Raised by sharks, he became very self-confident. And he winds up being half boy, half shark, occasionally going into these shark frenzies, where he starts biting and ripping stuff. He gets really, really crazy. And that's when you don't want to be near him.

'But he was fun to play because he got to do a lot of acrobatic stuff. And he gets to move like a shark and throw lots and lots of temper tantrums!'

Taylor was a big fan of Rodriguez's smart *Spy Kids* movies, so he was delighted to be working with the director. 'I was definitely familiar with the *Spy Kids* movies, because I loved all three of them and watched them a lot. And my mom heard a lot of great stuff about him, so when I booked the movie and I heard I got to work with him, I was really excited. When we got there, I saw why.

'He was so much fun. One, he's great to be around because he plays video games with you. He's also a great director, because we were shooting on green screen for 90 per cent of the movie and he helped us a lot. He'd tell us, "OK, this is over here and this is over there. This is what it looks like." Everybody loved to work with Robert.'

It was a dream role for Taylor because he got to spend his day doing what he loves the most – acting and doing action scenes. 'I got to be a superhero and everything's fun when you get to be a superhero. You get to do a lot of stunts… and lots of kids love doing stunts because you get to do wirework, and you get to do a lot of fun stuff on mats. And also because I got to wear a cool suit, and that suit was very awesome. So there's lots of cool reasons for being a superhero.'

Taylor spent three months working on the movie in Robert Rodriguez's usual shooting location – Austin, Texas. Ironically, the director didn't know the full extent of Taylor's martial arts training and was stunned when he asked the young actor to show off some moves. Suitably impressed, he asked Taylor to choreograph the fight scenes in the film.

Taylor explains, 'While we were in Austin, he saw a DVD of me and asked me to choreograph my own fight scenes. So I used all my martial arts to do stuff on the green screen, and he said, "If it works then we can put it in the movie and if not, not." But he loved it, so, using his magical powers, he put those people who I was fighting in and it worked just like I was fighting those plugs with my martial arts.'

Talking about the shooting schedule, Taylor revealed to *ultimatedisney.com*, 'Ninety per cent of it was done on green screen. We just had three days at a house, three days at a school and that was about it. All the other 55 days were on the green screen.'

It may have been his biggest acting role to date, but there were no nerves from Taylor and he certainly made an impression on the set of the film. The young actor was a constant whirlwind of energy, alongside his two young co-stars Taylor Dooley (Lavagirl) and Cayden Boyd, who plays Max the dreamer.

'We had a lot of fun on the set. After we were done shooting, the three of us would go behind the set and play hide'n'seek and climb trees. We had so much fun on the set. And we all see each other a lot since we live only a few blocks from one another. We go out to dinner together and we have many of our friends from the set over for sleepovers.'

Proof that it's a small world, Dooley also happened to hail from Grosse Point, near Detroit in Michigan, and she and Taylor only lived a few blocks apart in LA. Talking to *Reel Answers*, he explained, 'It's really weird. Our moms have the same name, we both have younger siblings, and we live practically across the street from each other in

LA. If I were to drive to her house, it would take only take seconds!'

However, there were complications. Because they both shared the same first name, the crew needed to give them nicknames. 'At first on set it was very confusing having the same name as Taylor Dooley. After a while everyone just started calling us "Sharky" or "Lava". That helped a lot! Ha ha!'

The pair would remain close afterwards, often making home movies together. Because not only did Taylor want to star in films, he wanted to direct as well, after enjoying every minute of the experience working with Robert Rodriguez.

'I would love to go the acting route,' he revealed while promoting the film, 'but if I couldn't, I would want to be like Robert Rodriguez, a writer and director. Because I do a lot of home movies with Taylor Dooley and her younger brother. We make a lot of films together and we're actually in the middle of one right now. So, we have a lot of fun doing that. I'd really love to do that if the acting thing didn't work out.'

He added to *Popcorn*, 'I do love making movies with my video camera and my editing system on my laptop. Usually the movies are all action! Some of them are mysteries or kidnaps... stuff like that. I think it is a good way to learn and it's also fun.'

It's still true for him now. 'I also love writing and directing,' he told *Interview* magazine in 2009. 'I'd love to get into that. Right now I'm an actor. But I could see that in my future.'

In another interview he added, 'I would love to do an extreme action movie and choreograph my own stunts. That's actually been like a dream film of mine since I started acting.'

Also appearing in *The Adventures of Sharkboy and Lavagirl* was *Scream* actor David Arquette, husband of *Friends* actress Courtney Cox. Unfortunately for young Taylor, he hardly got to see the comedy actor in action.

'We didn't get to see him that much because while he was on the set – we were in school. For the most part, he seemed very, very quiet. And very, very nice, always cracking jokes on the set. While the jokes would go along with the individual scenes, nobody would be able to stop laughing and they'd always have to start over.'

Rodriguez made sure the atmosphere was an enjoyable one for the young cast, to ensure they didn't get bored waiting for each shot to be set up. 'Everybody loved working with him,' said Taylor. 'He played video games with us on the set. For instance, while I'd be shooting a particular scene, he'd be off playing video games with Taylor [Dooley]. It was so much fun.'

It wasn't all fun and games however. Because he was so young, Taylor still had to go to school – in this case in the form of an on-set tutor. Not surprisingly, that wasn't so attractive to Taylor. 'My least favourite part was the three hours of school on the set every day. School is good, but it's not really fun. If it had to be anything, it would have to be that!'

One thing he definitely did enjoy, however, was filming the scenes in the Land of the Milk and Cookies world. 'One of them is when we're on the giant cookie and I got to step in a big puddle of chocolate and then I got to eat it. And I also liked getting whipped cream and ice cream all over us 'cause that was fun.

'It was real chocolate and then the ice cream was actually just coloured whipped cream. Because we land on the cake, and there's supposed to be frosting and ice cream and we've got whipped cream on us. Those were probably my favourite couple of scenes.'

The film also gave Taylor the chance to attend a premiere of his own film at a very young age. He wouldn't know it but it was to be something that he would have to get used to in the near future.

'But walking the red carpet, you wouldn't believe how many photographers are there!' he told journalists at the event. '"Taylor, turn over here! Turn to the right! Hold it there! To the left! Now over here!" It's really crazy on the red carpet, but knowing that it was your premiere made it even more fun.'

The first time Taylor saw the movie was at a

screening for the cast and crew. 'It was as different as I thought it would be,' he said. 'But it was fun watching how much fun we had on the set and how it turned out as a movie. It made me think of all the memories and moments from all the different scenes we shot.'

The Adventures of Sharkboy and Lavagirl wasn't well received, however. The BBC called it a 'ceaselessly inventive but ultimately tedious caper set in a three-dimensional CG world' before going on to say, 'Unfortunately, there's no rhyme or reason to the delirious imagery put before us. Nor are the leads surrounded by the kind of stellar ensemble that made the *Spy Kids* films as enjoyable for adults as they were for kids. *Shark Boy* works fine as a Ritalin substitute for kids with ADHD. Their mums and dads, though, will be reaching for the paracetamol.' Ouch!

Despite the reviews, working on the movie gave Taylor increased confidence that he was good enough to make a career out of acting. Hollywood is littered with thousands of wannabes dreaming of making it big but failing. Taylor had the same dreams, but after his first starring role, he quickly found himself working alongside Steve Martin in his next movie, *Cheaper by the Dozen 2*. In it he played Eliot, the son of the Bakers' new rivals, the Murtaughs.

'It's about a disorganised family, Steve Martin's family,' he explained. 'And they have competitions with this new family that they meet on summer vacation. We're this straight-A, athletic, organised family and we just have all these competitions like canoeing and jet skiing.'

One of the advantages of working with a large group of young actors was that he was never lonely on set. 'I really got along with everyone on set. During filming I would spend most of my time hanging out with my film brothers and sisters, but off set I hung out with Alyson Stoner [his girlfriend Sarah in the movie] and a bunch of others. Alyson and I played a lot of ping-pong in our down time. It was a lot of fun though, because I was never bored because there were always 20 kids to play with.'

It also gave Taylor a chance to work alongside a genuine comedy legend in Steve Martin. 'It was an awesome opportunity to work with Steve. He was always nice to the kids, making sure he talked to everyone. Besides being nice, he is also an excellent role model on being prepared and working hard.'

Taylor was now a bona fide movie star. 'Ten-year-old boys were the ones who first recognised me,' he recalled. 'I'd be in the store, and boys would whisper to their moms. Then the moms would say, "Excuse me, are you Sharkboy?" I just thought it was so cool. I couldn't believe people wanted my picture.'

More than 10-year-old boys would want his picture after his next big role. It was to be a film that flew under the radar of most movie critics. But as soon as the ardent fans of a book series heard a film was to be made about it, they would propel the movie from its predicted cult following into the mainstream. The name of the film was *Twilight* and Taylor had no idea how much the character of Jacob Black was going to change his life.

chapter three
Twilight

'Jacob is an ordinary kid who has to deal with extraordinary things that he wasn't prepared for.' – Stephenie Meyer

*T*wilight came to Stephenie Meyer in a dream. 'I had a dream about a vampire and a woman talking in a meadow. It came from nowhere. Once I started I didn't need another dream. The story wrote itself,' she said, in the *Twilight* DVD documentary *A Conversation with Stephenie Meyer*.

'2 June 2003: I know the exact day that I woke up from the dream and started writing,' she added. 'It sounds cheesy but it was a great dream. The meadow scene in the movie is basically the dream that I had. When I woke up, I wanted to know what happened to those characters.

'I was so afraid that I would forget this great dream that I wrote ten pages, pretty much the whole of chapter 13, and then after that I just wanted to know what happened. I didn't expect to write a novel – just a chance to play with the characters in my head. When I finished it no one was more shocked than me to see I had finished a book.'

Twilight is told from the perspective of Bella, a 17-year-old teenager who is forced to move from her mother's home of Scottsdale in sunny Arizona to her father's rain-drenched world in the small town of Forks, Washington. After enrolling in the local high school and making a small group of friends, she is intrigued by the Cullen clan – a group of impossibly attractive boys and girls. Then Edward, constantly described as the most beautiful person ever, appears and the pair embark on a passionate, dramatic and dangerous romance.

The result of Stephenie's dream went on to become a massive success, debuting at number five on the *New York Times* bestseller list before peaking at number one. It was the bestselling book of 2008 and spawned three other books in a series – *New Moon*, *Eclipse* and *Breaking Dawn*. Together, the four books have sold more than 70 million copies worldwide, with at least 38 different translations around the world.

But even before the book's massive success, Meyer's vision was already being earmarked for a Hollywood makeover. In fact, it hadn't even been published when it fell into the hands of a very important person.

The film's producer Greg Mooradian said in the *Twilight* production notes, 'Part of my job as a producer is to scour the world for new material. I read a lot of manuscripts prior to their being published. When this one came across my desk, I just couldn't put it down. The premise of a girl falling in love with a vampire just hit me like a ton of bricks. And the book delivered on every level.

'There have been thousands of vampire films made. What sets this apart is the love story. Vampirism in this story is simply a metaphor for teenage lust, for that feeling "I want you but I can't have you." I thought that was such a wonderful metaphor to express teenage longing.'

He went on to add in another interview, 'There is no way to predict the life of a book. You have to go with your instinct. Often, when I'm reading a young adult book, I have to imagine whether a 15-year-old girl might enjoy reading it. What struck me in my initial reading of the *Twilight* manuscript was how much I enjoyed it, how completely absorbing it was, even while knowing I was far afield of who the book was supposed to speak to. My reaction told me this was more than a book for a young girl. This was a first-time author's unedited novel, but I was able to see past [its raw quality] because the themes of the story and the characters were so wonderful.

'It had universal themes, like *Romeo and Juliet*, which certainly influenced this book. It struck me this was a great movie premise – it seemed the greatest idea nobody had ever done. But at the time there was no way to predict it would connect with every young girl in America the way it has, that it would become an anthem for young girls as much as anything in contemporary culture.'

Some writers are tremendously precious about letting their book be adapted for the screen, but there was no such attitude from Meyer. 'When I was writing the novel I saw it as a movie. It was a very visual experience so I really wanted to see it brought to life,' she explained.

Being a film fan, she was aware that some things in the book would have to be changed for the big screen, but as long as they kept the core elements they could do what they want. 'All of us have seen books ruined as movies and I had a lot of things I wanted to protect. My stipulations were very basic: "You can't kill anyone who doesn't die in the book. The Cullens have to all exist by their right names and in their right characters." Things like that. I wanted the groundwork to be there.'

But Meyer's delight that her book was being turned into a movie turned into sorrow when, as often happens to potential movies, the idea languished in Development Hell – a term used for a film idea that has been bought by a studio but is struggling to get made.

It had all looked so promising when Paramount's

then president Karen Rosenfelt agreed to make the movie though the company's MTV Films division. 'Greg was so passionate and ready to dive on his sword, knowing this would be a franchise both for publishing and for film,' she said.

A writer was brought in to work on the screenplay, but production was halted when Rosenfelt left the company. Enter Summit Entertainment. They were very much in the early stages of becoming their own film company, so something like *Twilight* must have been like a gift that fell on their laps. Here was a book that was about to become a publishing phenomenon – a story that had romantic elements for the girls and a supernatural one for the boys. But it would still have been a hard sell if it wasn't for the perseverance of Mooradian.

'*Twilight* got out of its limbo state because Greg as a producer was so extraordinarily passionate about it and always beating the drum on it,' Rosenfelt remembered. 'I had a meeting with Erik Feig, the president of Summit, and he asked me if there was any project he should chase that Paramount might let go of. I told him the one he should get hold of is *Twilight*.'

Twilight fans may have had to wait a little bit longer to get one of their favourite books on the big screen, but it was worth the wait compared to what might have been if the MTV version was ever made. Catherine Hardwicke, who would direct the film, said of the early script, '*Twilight* was fascinating to me, but on the opening page, Bella is introduced as a star athlete – she's like a track star.'

Not a great start. 'Bella is clumsy, she's not an athlete, she's awkward,' Hardwicke continued. 'She's like every other girl, that's why we relate to her. By the end of that script it was like *Charlie's Angels* with the FBI and jet ski. I said to Summit, you guys have to make it like the book. So we went back to Stephenie's book.'

If Meyer was at all worried about the fate of her debut novel, she needn't have been. With Hardwicke in charge her baby was in safe hands. 'We just took the book into film language,' Hardwicke explained. 'The novel has to go through the condensing machine for a movie; we had to boil it down to its essence.

'In a movie we can show more action, so my goal was to make it a little less internal. If there was a passive scene, we tried to find ways to make it visually active. Stephenie gave us a lot of awesome notes. She has a feeling for things Bella would feel and say better than anyone else. In the screenplay, Stephenie also got to address tiny technical things she might have changed in her first novel.'

Hardwicke also ensured that Meyer was involved in all aspects of the production. 'My experience with Catherine has been wonderful,' said Meyer. 'I have this sense that she really has my back on this. She has kept the vision of the book and has kept everything in line.'

Screenwriter Melissa Rosenberg added, 'When she [Meyer] went to Summit and they convinced her to let them option it, she insisted on a series of things that absolutely had to be in the book: things that could not be changed. For instance, the characters had to be the same, the vampires had to have the same skills and same limitations. We had this manifesto we started with that was a couple of pages long. They sent it to me and I thought there was absolutely nothing on that manifesto that would hamper me. We've all had favourite books adapted for the screen then say, "Why did they do that?"'

Luckily for Meyer, she loved every minute of translating the book to the screen, although she did put her foot down on one occasion – insisting that Kellan Lutz should be cast as Emmett.

'My personality is such that I have a really hard time being critical with other people. I can be critical of myself all day long. But I hate to step in and say, "I really wish this was different." But it's been good for me just in general to have to speak up because I am so invested in this. I've forced myself, like with the Emmett situation, to take a step forward and say, "I don't like this." That's hard for me, but I'm glad of every time I did it and I don't think I stepped on too many toes and everyone seems to still like me.'

There was one moment in particular that she will

never forget – the day she met the actors who would turn her characters into flesh and blood.

'It was really surreal,' she recalled. 'The first night I was on set, I went to dinner and it was the first time I had met any of the cast. They came straight in from a photo shoot, so they were in costume. And there is nothing in the world like sitting down at a table with a bunch of people who are people you made up. It was just bizarre. And they looked amazing. I don't think I ate the whole time I was there, because I was so keyed up and nervous.'

While *Twilight* has a romantic hero in Edward Cullen, it was always Jacob that Meyer had a soft spot for. 'Jacob is an ordinary kid who has to deal with extraordinary things that he wasn't prepared for,' she said. 'I love Jacob. Because he's such a 16-year-old boy. I just love him as a character. He's become such a bigger part of the story because I had such a soft spot for him. I have been surrounded by boys, with my kids, my brothers, my father and uncles, so he was very familiar to write about.'

Meyer says that the two male characters are more similar than people realise. 'Jacob and Edward are similar in that they both want to be good people. They try their hardest to do their best, to do everything that's important to them.

'They're not similar in that Edward is very careful – he weighs everything before he acts, whereas Jacob is very impetuous. Whatever comes to mind, he does it. It's a very human mistake and he's fine with that. He's open to it, he moves on and gets on with it. Edward dwells on things and anguishes over it, while Jacob lets it go.'

In a press release of 16 November 2007, Summit Entertainment announced to the world: 'We at Summit are truly excited about the franchise potential of this remarkable Romeo and Juliet story. Of course, you are only as good as your Juliet and Kristen Stewart has that magical combination of being a great actress, deeply appealing, and perfect for the part.'

A month later they announced the casting of Edward Cullen. Erik Feig, Summit Entertainment's President of Production, stated, 'It's always a challenge to find the right actor for a part that has lived so vividly in the imaginations of readers but we took the responsibility seriously and are confident, with Rob Pattinson, that we have found the perfect Edward for our Bella in *Twilight*.'

While the casting of Jacob Black wasn't heralded with the same fanfare as Edward and Bella, Taylor was delighted to get the part. He would only appear in a handful of scenes in this first film, but fans of the series knew his role was going to get bigger and bigger. But that was the future. Taylor was just determined to do the best job possible for this one.

chapter four
Jacob Black

'This is life-changing.' – Taylor Lautner

Jacob is introduced early on in the film, showing Bella her present from her dad – a battered orange truck. It's clear from the start that he has held a crush on her for a long time.

He is also the first to hint to Bella that there may be more to Edward than meets the eye, while at the same acknowledging a mystery past of his own, mainly that the Cullen family and his Quileute tribe have a rivalry that spans decades. Unknown to Bella, Jacob has his own supernatural ability – he is a werewolf.

It was the character's unique dual personality that really thrilled Taylor. 'His Native American side ... he is very friendly and outgoing. He loves Bella and is very loyal to Bella and his dad. But on the werewolf side, they're very fierce and just attacking, and they have this huge temper,' he told MTV. 'So there's a lot of stress and things going on inside him as he's trying to keep his temper to himself. I love that part, which Stephenie created, with the contrast between the Native American side and the werewolf side of him.'

When Taylor bagged the role of Jacob, *Twilight* fans expressed concerns about the part being given to him. However, they – and he – soon learned that he had Native American blood in him. 'We learned that through [preparing for] this film. I'm French, Dutch and German, and on my mother's side, she has some Potawatomi and Ottawa Indian in her.'

Taylor was so desperate to do the part justice that he made sure he did his research. 'When I first went up to Portland to film, I met with some real Quileute Native Americans,' he revealed to *MediaBlvd Magazine*. 'We went out to dinner with them and got a chance to talk to them. The funny thing I learned is that they're just like me. They showed up in basketball uniforms. Somehow, we got on the topic of what they like to do for fun, and they go to the beach and check out girls. It was really interesting to learn that they're just like me.

'One thing I noticed is they don't need to be told to what to do,' he added to MTV. 'If the trash is getting full, they empty it out. They're always helping each other. They're always there for each other. So I just want to make sure I can bring that part of Jacob alive.'

In doing so Taylor became incredibly close to the character. '[The werewolf side] is not like me in real life,' he said. 'I'm like Jacob's Native American side. I'm very friendly, outgoing, energetic and easy to talk to. But playing the werewolf side, where he's holding all this anger and stuff inside him, that'd be very different for me. I love to challenge myself as an actor.'

There were some reports that the Native American tribe – who number nearly 400 members on a reservation at La Push, Washington – were less than happy with their portrayal in the film, which sees them change from humans to wolves.

When he went to audition for the film, Taylor admitted that he had no idea what he was getting himself in for. 'When I first found out I had an audition for some *Twilight* movie, my agent told me, like, "Yeah, this one's kind of big." And I was like, "I've never heard of it."

'So I go in on it, and yeah, the director's really cool. I go back and I read with Kristen Stewart and she's really cool. Still I have no idea what the project is about or how big it is. So then I get cast and I go do my research. "Oh, this is based off a book series. How big is the book series?"

'So I check it out and it's just mind-blowing. I'm just, "Oh my gosh, what am I getting myself into? This is life changing."'

In an interview with *Grand Rapids Press*, he added, 'I realised how big it was. Suddenly, it was all over the Internet. I started hearing about all the hype, all the fans. I thought, "Oh my goodness. If I get this, it'll be huge. I really want this."'

When Taylor signed on soon afterwards, he was used to working with people his age on his movies. Now, at 16, he was one of the youngest members of the cast. He began to worry whether or not the older members would hang out with a teenager. He needn't have worried, however.

'At first I was a little bit nervous about that but if you think about it, I'm only a year and a half younger than Kristen. But the cast is really friendly and we all had great chemistry and we all got along. I honestly don't feel the age difference.'

The older cast members embraced Taylor and always made him feel welcome. But during the first film, the cast didn't socialise as much as they wanted, as they were too busy with their hectic filming schedule. 'Most of our time, we wake up bright and early, go film until six o'clock at night, so all we had time for was go back, get a bite to eat together and hit the hay for the next day. It was quite fun, though: the cast is awesome.'

In *Twilight* Taylor's main scenes are with Kristen, so it's no surprise he bonded with her the most. 'The only people who were there when I was on set were Kristen and Rob, and he wasn't there too much. So it was basically just me and Kristen. She's very easy going. It takes her a little bit to warm up to people. She's a little shy and reserved. Her and Rob both are. But she was very fun to be around.'

There was one small scene in the film that could have proved to be a stumbling block for the character. His part required driving the family's beat-up truck. The only problem was that Taylor couldn't drive. He soon got his licence but he was still nervous, as he had only learned how to drive using newer cars. 'I've got my licence in my back pocket to show them I'm OK and that I won't kill them... hopefully!' he joked to MTV. 'I'm going to test out driving Bella's truck and my family's truck. One of them is an automatic, so that will be nice and easy. The other one has no power steering, so I'll have to muscle it. That will be interesting. I've never done that before.

'It's really old and beat-up, and that's the one without the power steering. So I'm going to be driving with my dad right next to me. We want to make sure I get used to it, so it looks natural.'

Another aspect that caused Taylor some grief was his long flowing wig. 'The costume and wardrobe were the easiest part,' he told *Vanity Fair* magazine. 'The most difficult part for me was the wig. It took a while to put on and take off.'

In another interview, he explained, 'Taking it off was kind of easier, but putting it on was quite a bit more difficult. We had many steps and stages. When I first heard I was going to be wearing a wig, I was excited. I was like, "Cool, I've never worn a wig before! This is going to be awesome!"

'But sure enough, after the first day of filming, I was through with the wig! It was itchy and it was always getting into my face when I was trying to eat and saying my lines and talking to Kristen.'

It took him a while to get used to his new look, he told *movies.about.com*. 'I've never had my hair longer than it is right now, so just looking at myself like that is like, "Wow, do I look like a girl? I do look like a girl, ah!"'

But mostly Taylor had a great time on set, although he did notice a few differences that made *Twilight* stand out from his other films.

'The thing I thought was interesting about the weather was that, usually on film sets, when it starts raining they have to call "Cut!" and wait for the rain to stop. But for *Twilight*, it was the opposite. There was one scene that was just supposed to be a normal walk on the beach with Bella, and it turned out that there was a hurricane-tornado warning with hail, sleet, snow and freezing rain, and the tide was up to our knees. So, the weather was difficult.'

It was more than difficult. Shooting the scene where Bella goes to the beach to meet her friends and ends up finding out about the Cullen history through Jacob, has entered into legend with the cast and crew – all eager to share their stories of the horrendous weather.

In the official book companion to the movie, director Catherine Hardwicke recalled, 'First, the crew bus was slowed down for an hour driving through a snowstorm on a mountain road. Then the equipment had to be hauled by hand down a rocky beach. Then it rained non-stop – freezing, 45-degree-angle rain. The camera crew, clad head to toe in Gore-Tex, wrapped the camera bodies completely in plastic and we tried to shoot anyway.

'Now the crew had to hike back cross the rocks with their equipment in the pouring rain, which took an hour and a half, to find a lunch tent that was literally blowing away. The crew and various reporters [who had come to visit] had to hold it down. Meanwhile, the nearly horizontal freezing rain continued. I was told I had to shoot the beach surf vans and arranged them in the parking lot to block the wind, and had Bella and Angela play the scene sitting in the van. It was miserable and many of the crew complained about "inhuman conditions". But we got the scene... barely.

'The next day, one of the producers congratulated me on making the day, saying, "No other director that I know would have kept shooting in those conditions." I was thinking, "You mean I had a choice?"'

Taylor recalled, 'We showed up for the beach

scene, where Jacob is just supposed to take his wannabe girlfriend Bella for a nice walk on the beach. And it was 40mph winds, hail, rain...

'Wardrobe had originally picked out just jeans and a T-shirt for us, and when we show up it's pouring rain, sleet and hail the size of golf balls. So we ended up wearing three pairs of pants, raincoats, rain pants, beanies, everything possible. I'll always remember it.

'It was my least favourite scene because it was kind of hard to act in. You're trying to be all serious walking her and you're almost falling over because of the wind, golf ball-size hail balls – but at the same time, it was kind of fun. It was an adventure.'

He did feel sorry for Kristen however, and not just because of the weather conditions. As she was one of the younger members of the cast, she had to get a tutor while filming. The tutor worked out of a local high school. 'I had to go to school in this school,' Kristen recalled. 'While we were shooting I had to use one of the classrooms. We put paper over the little class portal so people couldn't see through because people kept banging on the door. I felt like a monkey in a cage.'

Speaking on the film's commentary, Hardwicke added, 'Kristen was a minor – she had to go to school for 20 minutes, film an intense scene...'

Taylor was sympathetic, as he had to regularly do that as well. 'You gotta do school three hours a day and sometimes more, because they want to "bank" hours. At the end of the movie, if you don't have enough time or if you want to relax more, you're going to be leaving in a couple of days, then you get to use some of your bank hours. That's pretty much how it works.'

Taylor made such a big impact on set that it wasn't long after the first cut that he was asked to shoot more scenes. 'Well, I am going to be in the prom scene now, at the very end of the film,' he told journalists during the reshoots. 'At first we didn't film that, and now some people are saying they want to see a bit more of Jacob, and they want him in the prom scene at the end.'

The prom scene at the end is what excited Taylor and fans of the series, as it hints at the potential love triangle between Edward, Jacob and Bella.

When Jacob tries to warn Bella to be careful, Edward cuts in and leads Bella to the prom. 'I leave you alone for two minutes, they send the wolves out,' he states wryly.

Hardwicke explained, 'When we put the film together we realised you are missing Jacob at the end so we put together a short scene but it's important, because you still get a taste of that rivalry between him and Edward.'

Filming that scene was something of a vindication for Taylor, as he had pleaded with Hardwicke to put it in when he realised his favourite scene from the book hadn't made it into the original script. 'When I read the script I was like, "Really? He doesn't come to the prom?"' he told *movies.about.com*. 'I think I asked Catherine about it and I forgot what she said. But I was just like, "Oh, OK…" But sure enough, you know, they were like, "OK, we're doing it."'

When final shoots and editing were completed, Meyer was delighted with what she saw in a pre-release viewing. 'I was terrified for days in advance before I saw *Twilight* for the first time. I was so worried that it was going to be horrible and break my heart. I'd seen things that were really good, but for all the time I'd spent on the set, I'd probably seen ten minutes of the movie altogether. So I asked if it was OK if some of my friends watch with me because I have these great friends who are really positive and they love everything!

'I was really worried about it but we got in there and they put it on. I had my paper and my pen because it was a rough cut and I wanted to give feedback on things I felt needed to be changed. And I didn't write a single thing down because I was so involved. The characters were speaking the way they should and the heart was there. I could have watched it all night in a loop if I could have.'

But there were still worries at Summit because, despite the hype, it was by no means a guaranteed winner. At the time, the books had sold well, but they weren't in the region of Dan Brown's *The Da*

Vinci Code or JK Rowling's *Harry Potter* books just yet. And there was the nagging worry that the film would not appeal to boys. As a rival studio insider said, 'If they just get teenage girls they're dead.'

'If I were marketing this movie,' said pop culture professor Robert Thompson, 'I'd want to make sure it doesn't look like it's based on the books, because anyone who reads the books is already in the tent. Make it look like a rip-roaring good story about vampires that doesn't make a 12-year-old boy say, "That's what the girls are reading."'

On its release, too, the reviews were decidedly mixed. 'Too brooding to be camp, too silly to be taken seriously, *Twilight* sits right on the edge of being either good trash or an allegorical tale of teenage passion,' said *chud.com*. 'The movie is filled with dialogue that beggars belief and performances driven more by haircuts than by any school of acting. Worst of all, it's cheap, a budget production from top to bottom. This is certainly going to be the thriftiest blockbuster since *The Blair Witch Project*.' But the naysayers were proved spectacularly wrong at the box office. *Twilight* was a huge success, taking nearly $70 million in its opening weekend alone. Robert Pattinson insists he'd always had an inkling that the film was going to be a big hit. 'I don't really think even the production company knew how big it was going to become. It's interesting, but as we were shooting it sort of got bigger and bigger and bigger, and more and more people started turning up to the set every day.'

Peter Facinelli, who plays Carlisle Cullen, had no idea, however. 'When we first shot it, I think no one really knew that it was going to be this big. I think we were just hoping to satisfy the fans of the books, and we knew there was this underground following. Again, no one really knew it was going to snowball into this huge thing.'

When *Twilight* was issued on DVD in the US, its success was underlined all over again. It sold more than three million copies on its first day of release – a staggering amount.

When Taylor had done a little digging on the Internet before his audition, he had had a feeling that this role, if he got it, was going to change his life. He was right, and then some.

chapter five

Twilight Shines Bright

'The fans are driving this thing.' – Taylor Lautner

Before *Twilight*, Taylor had still been in the public eye thanks to the success of *Sharkboy and Lavagirl*, and was seen as something of a role model to young boys. While promoting that film, he said, 'All my fans have been really supportive and encouraging. It means a lot to me when parents have said to me that they appreciate the role model they feel I am to their kids. I love little kids and when parents feel good about who they look up to, that makes me feel good inside.'

His *Twilight* character is much loved by the series' fans, prompting many arguments as to which Team you support – Team Jacob or Team Edward. But even Taylor wasn't to know how big the support was until they went to San Diego's Comic Con event to give fans a sneak preview. The *Twilight* presentation was hands down the biggest hit of 2008.

Fans turned up in thousands and screamed the place down. It was only then that the cast realised what they had let themselves in for. Even when they were introduced one by one to the audience the screams were deafening. Each answer was greeted with rapturous applause, no matter how mundane the replies were to the many questions.

'We got there and it was huge.' Taylor recalled. 'Just coming out onstage and hearing everyone scream and seeing how many people were in that auditorium was crazy.'

Speaking to the *LA Times*, he added, 'I've never seen anything like it before. We were all pretty nervous but once we got out there it was pretty fun – at least for me. The fans are just very passionate and really excited for the movie to come out.'

And when the film was released, the screaming fans only got louder. 'It is insane, but they are so supportive,' he said. 'I don't think there are better fans out there.'

Taylor's kind words were 100 per cent genuine. At the film's LA premiere in November 2008, he was left speechless at the reception he and his castmates received. 'I left my brain at the door. It's completely insane. You never expect it... I'm completely deaf,' he joked. While his co-stars Robert Pattinson and Kristen Stewart looked dumbfounded at the reception, Taylor soaked it up like an old pro.

For Taylor it was one of the best nights of his life, and he chose to share it with a member of his family rather than just some nice-looking girl on his arm. It was the right thing to do for all the support his family had given him for chasing that dream – a dream that was now being fully realised.

'I invited a lot of people,' he said, 'but I'm having one of my grandparents come out for the movie and they're actually going to the premiere. All of my family lives in Michigan and every family member has read the books. I mean, all four of my grandparents, aunts and uncles, everybody! It's just crazy cool that they love it so much.'

And the fans love Taylor, although being called a heartthrob in the press is a tag he has not quite got used to. 'Oh boy – I'm not sure,' he told *alloy.com*. 'It's a little scary. I don't know – I wouldn't call [me] a teen heartthrob, would I? The fans behind this are great, so I'm very excited to be involved with this project. It's so cool. I've seen the movie, it's awesome. The fans are awesome, the cast and crew are awesome, so I'm definitely stoked to be part of it.

'I don't know if it's really hit me yet. They're just passionate for the series and for the characters, and we're just lucky enough to be a part of this. I don't think it has much to do with me personally; it's more because I'm playing the beloved Jacob Black,' he added.

Twilight's success has also benefited the real-life town of Forks, giving it a much-needed economic boost. 'The town was having some major economic issues, because their major export was logging – and then *Twilight* came along,' said *Twilight* blogger Kaleb Nation. 'And if you look at Forks now, Stephenie has transformed this town into a *Twilight* tourism economy. It's crazy.'

Tens and tens of thousands of fans have descended on the town in a bid to savour the atmosphere of the book's setting, although the film wasn't actually shot there. Forks Visitor Center's Marcia Binham said, 'What a gift this has been.'

Binham, who makes sure that all her staff are *Twilight* fluent, can't believe the attention, noting that it's come a long way from the days when they would spend their time telling tourists about the logging industry. She recalled that a girl had recently even asked them, 'Is it safe to go camping with the vampire problems in the area?'

One fan event in the summer of 2009 saw the town transformed into the world of the series. 'Forks: a *Twilight* Symposium' gave *Twilight* fans the chance to attend classes at Forks high school, eat a meal where the characters eat and attend the school prom like Edward and Bella at the end of *Twilight*. Shops were emblazoned with cardboard cut outs of

Pattinson and Stewart, and signs that read 'Edward Cullen Slept Here'.

For a young boy from Michigan, Taylor can't believe the attention he receives. Every day there will be a constant visual reminder that his life has changed forever: scores of female teenagers wearing T-shirts emblazoned with his image and the words: Team Jacob. 'It's weird to see my character's name on other people's bodies,' he recalled to *MediaBlvd Magazine*. 'I guess it can get a little nerve-wracking at some points, but it's just exciting for me, knowing how much the fans support this, and knowing how passionate and dedicated they are.'

Asked if he follows what's said about him on the web, he replied, 'I read it sometimes. I'm not on the Internet 24/7 going, "Ooh, what are they saying about me? What's the latest stuff?" But, sometimes I run into stuff, and I do check out some of the fan sites for the book. The fans are driving this thing.'

One fan encounter left the actor blushing. 'I had this 40-year-old woman trying to find a way to take her panties off for me to sign them. They had my name imprinted on them. So that was kind of strange. But you can't expect anything less from these *Twilight* fans.

'One of the other weirdest fan things is somebody sent me a link and said, "What is this?" And it was a picture of women's underwear being sold online with "Taylor" written on it. So it was kind of weird to have women's underwear with my name imprinted on the front.

'It's funny, but about a year ago I'd talk to girls and no one would be interested. Then when it was announced I would be in *Twilight* and everyone seemed to change their mind,' he said.

But as much as he's forever grateful for his fans' support and attention, there is one question that drives him howling mad. 'I'm asked to growl by fans. And I really don't like doing that. Please don't ask me to growl, just wait for the movie [*New Moon*].'

chapter six

Taylor's Twilight Begins to Fade

'As far as I know, I haven't been told "no" yet, so it's still all up in the air.'
Taylor Lautner

Not only was Taylor starring in *Twilight* but he was making waves on the small screen as well, after grabbing the role of Christian Slater's son in the TV show *My Own Worst Enemy*.

It was a role he was clearly excited about. 'Christian Slater's character has two lives: He's like the clumsy family man, and then in his other life, he's like this assassin super spy. I have the blood of his assassin side. They don't know where it comes from. All of a sudden, I'm this star soccer player, and I'm really good at martial arts.'

The press release for the show gives the following synopsis: 'Henry Spivey (Slater) is a middle-class efficiency expert living a humdrum life in the suburbs with his wife, Lily (Yara Martinez), their two kids, a dog, and a minivan. Edward Albright (Slater) is an operative who speaks 13 languages, runs a four-minute mile, and is trained to kill.'

The two people are different parts of Albright's brain – and neither of them knows about the existence of each other thanks to a chip implant. However, when the chip in his brain malfunctions, forcing the two personas to swap with each other, things get very complicated indeed.

It had the potential to be an incredibly hectic period for Taylor as he had to juggle the roles of Jacob and Jack Spivey with school life. 'I film *My Own Worst Enemy* but that's only about two days a week,' he said.

Despite his protests, it was clear that he couldn't combine school life with his burgeoning film and TV career. In a 2008 interview with *Vanity Fair*, he said, 'I've always been in a public school until this year actually. I am working on a TV show on NBC, and I would be missing too much school. So I tested out of high school.'

Taylor is now taking college classes in his spare time – however little that is – in a bid to ensure he has a solid back-up plan if the acting career doesn't work out. It's another example of how Taylor was raised in a solid and grounded environment.

Despite the potential of *My Own Worst Enemy* and the lure of its leading man, the series was cancelled after only nine episodes. Still, Taylor was determined to make the most of the experience. Talking about the show, he has said, 'You know it was just really awesome to work with Christian Slater on that – he's such a great guy, so professional. I definitely learned a lot from him on that.'

It was no doubt a blow to Taylor but at that particular time he still couldn't believe his luck for being cast in the *Twilight* series. He loved the character of Jacob, and one line in *New Moon* in particular. 'It's not in the first book, but the quote I love the most is Jacob's quote, "Does my half being naked bother you?" That just cracks me up. Because you know, that's when he's shirtless, not wearing a top – we'll have to wait to see what he looks like. I am eager to say that line,' he grinned.

Joking aside, he was delighted to be part of the love triangle that still has fans arguing over who Bella should choose – the werewolf Jacob or the vampire Edward. And it's something that even Taylor can't decide.

'In the first movie, Jacob's hot, but Jacob won't live forever. You have people that say that it's cool to live forever, but he's more human-like than Edward. With the first movie, and the first book, you don't really know much. You just know that he's this really happy-go-lucky guy, who is just in love with Bella.'

Taylor wasn't to know it but his role of Jacob was less than secure. It may seem crazy now to even think that he was going to be replaced but it was definitely touch-and-go whether or not he would stay on.

Taylor was oblivious to the background drama; he just presumed he would be called back. When he had auditioned for *Twilight*, director Catherine Hardwicke had made sure he did a scene with Kristen Stewart to gauge their chemistry for later films. 'I originally met with Catherine and she wanted me to do a "chemistry test" with Kristen. We did a few scenes from the first book, like the beach scene, and then we read some lines straight out of the books *New Moon* and *Eclipse*.

'I don't remember the specific scenes, but I do know that the scenes I did showed a huge difference in Jacob's character. He goes from happy-go-lucky and friendly in *Twilight* to when he's more of a werewolf and more of an adult – all intense and grumpy. She wanted to see as much of me playing the different sides to Jacob as possible.'

Trouble first loomed when *Twilight* director Hardwicke was replaced. In a statement, she said, 'I am sorry that due to timing I will not have the opportunity to direct *New Moon*. Directing *Twilight* has been one of the great experiences of my life, and I am grateful to the fans for their passionate support of the film. I wish everyone at Summit the best with the sequel – it is a great story.'

Her exit was a huge shock to the series' fans as she had only recently begun disclosing her plans for *New*

Moon, and the success of *Twilight* made her the most successful female director on opening weekend ever.

This is what she said shortly before she left the production. 'Well, right now we're trying to figure out if the studio people, and me, and everyone's on the same page. I want to do better than we did *Twilight* and do it really cool. I definitely don't want to do it as something just seemingly tossed off, like a *Saw II* or something like that. We want to be sure that it's really going to be great.

'I would say that the film could be finished by the end of 2009, if not the beginning of 2010 – cameras could be rolling in about five months. We spent about a year and three months getting [*Twilight*] ready, between writing the script and casting. We could probably do things a little bit faster this time, but who knows? It depends. And sometimes you can do things really fast. You can get two editors on, and you can just zip through.'

The official reason for her exit was scheduling difficulties. Because of the huge success of *Twilight*, Summit were keen to get to work on the sequel as soon as possible. The company's President of Production, Erik Feig, said, 'Catherine did an incredible job in helping us to launch the *Twilight* franchise and we thank her for all of her efforts and we very much hope to work with her on future Summit projects.

'We as a studio have a mandate to bring the next

instalment in the franchise to the big screen in a timely fashion so that fans can get more of Edward, Bella and all of the characters that Stephenie Meyer has created. We are able to pursue an aggressive time frame as we have the luxury of only adapting the novels into screenplays as opposed to having to create a storyline from scratch.'

Despite Hardwicke and the studio's insistence that it was an amicable split, it was rumoured that Summit weren't impressed with her direction of *Twilight*. Certainly, it hadn't been the best-received movie by critics, though some had praised Hardwicke, saying that her involvement was the reason the film worked.

Tellingly, before her departure she answered a question about her involvement in the sequel with the words 'Where's my crystal ball? I need a crystal ball, I need a fortune teller. I hope so, but you just have to see if everything can work out. I don't know.'

However, she did go on to sign up for another Summit picture – an adaptation of Gayle Forman's children's book *If I Stay*. Feig said, 'When we were thinking of the perfect director to capture the emotion, grace, and passion of this beautiful book, one filmmaker became the clear and only choice: Catherine Hardwicke. Summit and Catherine have had enormous success working together on *Twilight* and we cannot wait to bring *If I Stay* to vivid life together as well.'

So it seems her departure from *Twilight* was more

amicable than first reported. And ironically she swapped vampires for wolves in another film she has planned, *The Girl With the Red Riding Hood*.

So out went Hardwicke – and in came Chris Weitz, director of *American Pie* and *The Golden Compass*. Summit's Feig beamed, 'We love Stephenie Meyer's fantastic *Twilight* series. Thinking long and hard about how to turn *New Moon* into the amazing movie we know it will be, and working with Stephenie Meyer to find the right candidate, we are thrilled to announce Chris Weitz as director of the film.

'Chris very much understands the world of *New Moon*, and has the skill set required to bring the book to glorious life as a movie. We think he will be an excellent steward of Stephenie Meyer's vision.'

Weitz was suitably deferential about his new employment. 'I am honoured to have been entrusted with shepherding *New Moon* from the page to the screen,' he said. 'The extraordinary world that Stephenie has created has millions of fans, and it will be my duty to protect on their behalf the characters, themes and story they love. This is not a task to be taken lightly, and I will put every effort into realising a beautiful film to stand alongside a beautiful book.'

To placate the fans angry about Hardwicke's departure, Weitz wrote on Meyer's website, 'When I saw the film of *Twilight*, I was alternately entranced and left hungry for more. I was also struck by the extraordinary passion for the characters, story and theme that was evident in the people sitting in the seats around me. My job is to live up that devotion.'

Meyer added, 'I've had the chance to talk to Chris, and I can tell you that he is excited by the story and eager to keep the movie as close to the book as possible.'

Talking to *Screen Fantasy* during a set visit of *New Moon*, Meyer added, 'I'm sad that Catherine Hardwicke is not continuing on with us for *New Moon*. I'm going to miss her, not just as a brilliant director but also as a friend. She has such a distinct, authentic voice that did amazing for us in *Twilight*. I'm looking forward to every movie she does in the future.

'Catherine didn't leave us empty handed. We still reap the benefits of her amazing casting and the beautiful visual world she created. The foundations put us in a good place for *New Moon*.'

All was well then for Meyer and Weitz, but less so for Taylor. Not until the change in directors did he begin to suspect that there might be trouble ahead. It seemed that the studio bosses feared that Taylor didn't have the physical requirements for the evolving story of Jacob – and these were not just slight concerns.

The film company's press release for *New Moon* pointedly left Taylor off the cast list. 'The casting decision in regards to the character Jacob Black has yet to be made,' was the blunt response when MTV News enquired about his omission.

This is what Taylor had to say when asked about the cast list. 'I think it's because, well, Rob and Kristen were the lead roles in *Twilight*, so they've got to be back. I don't know if they've officially signed – maybe they are, I don't know. They just hired Weitz, and now they're just moving down the cast. All I can say is, I'm going to be ready if my number's called.'

It seemed Summit had a list of actors lined up as replacements in case they decided not to stick with Taylor. One of them was *Scorpion King 2* actor Michael Copon. The actor was less than subtle about his desire to win the part, posting messages on his Facebook status like 'Michael Copon is in a *Twilight* Zone!' and 'Michael Copon is the older Jacob Black!'

It wasn't the first time that Taylor's slim frame had been talked about as hindering his chance of playing Jacob in future films. *Twilight* fans had already expressed their concerns over the matter – and Taylor was aware of it.

'In the first one, he's just regular and lanky and not crazy. But I'm sure after this one, I will be working out, eating my protein, and staying away from the ice cream and the sugar,' he promised.

Before Hardwicke's departure, Taylor had been thrilled to be working on the film, especially when the director was very vocal about his involvement in the sequel. Shortly before her departure she had said, 'I was doing a lot of research on wolves before [*Twilight*] and we had a scene with the wolves in it. So we're already thinking a little bit about [Jacob's transformation]. Then there's the stunts, and there's Italy [the next location]. It's all cooking in the brain.'

'The wolves will be tricky,' she continued, 'because they are supposed to be these giant wolves. Is it going to be CGI, real wolves or a combination? There are five standard industry ways of doing it. Which will be most effective? When you read the book, you see how quickly they transform, and you see the shredding clothes and the popping collars, so that's a challenge. How does that read on film? How does that translate to film? What you normally do is you do tests. You figure out some things that are working better, and things that are not working better. You try them out, hopefully, on real people.'

Talking about fears that Taylor wasn't in the right physical shape for Jacob for future instalments, she laughed. 'We are putting him on a medieval torture thing and stretching him. No, he's only 16, so he is still growing. His dad is tall, and he's working out, so you never know.'

She also had ideas on how to make the love triangle between Robert, Taylor and Kristen work. 'It will definitely be the challenge. That would be a thing to work on too. How do you deepen that chemistry and make it go to the next level?'

It had all looked so promising for Taylor, but now it seemed like he was to miss out just as his character was getting interesting. But Summit hadn't counted on the series' legion of hardcore fans, who were desperate to keep Taylor. One post from a fan summed up the majority of the fans' opinion. 'They cannot get rid of Taylor. I don't care if he'd be a short Jacob, they just can't get rid of him.

'He played a perfect Jacob. I mean, come on! Have you seen the guy they're thinking about replacing him with! Michael Copon is such a jerk, but Taylor is a big sweetheart. If they replace Taylor I'm not gonna see any more of the movies.'

Taylor's co-star Ashley Greene, who plays Alice Cullen, also fought his corner in public. 'We all love Taylor. He's such a sweet guy, so sweet and I think that he gets the part. And the thing is that the girls just love him. He is the teen heartthrob. [...] I'm hoping that they don't replace him because we love him.'

Summit also hadn't reckoned on Taylor's fighting spirit. He wasn't going to give up the role of a lifetime easily. Showing the same never-say-die attitude that won him all those martial arts championships years ago, he embarked on a serious, strenuous work-out regime to ensure that he matched the bulkier character described in the book. He pledged to Weitz that he would put on the muscle before filming began and diplomatically told MTV,

'I've heard a few things. I don't really know too much to comment on it. As far as I know, I haven't been told "no" yet, so it's still all up in the air.'

Talking to *Interview* magazine, he explained his gruelling work-out regime. 'My motivation is basically my passion for the character of Jacob and the series. I want the fans to be proud of the movie, so I have to live up to their Jacob.

'I was in the gym five days a week, two hours a day. At one point, I was going seven days straight. I had put on a lot of weight, and then I started losing it drastically, so I was worried. It turned out I was overworking myself. My trainer told me that I couldn't break a sweat, because I was burning more calories than I was putting on.

'The hardest thing for me was the eating. At one point I had to shove as much food in my body as possible to pack on the calories. My trainer wanted me to do six meals a day and not go two hours without eating. If I would cheat on eating one day, I could tell – I'd drop a few pounds.'

But Taylor's perseverance paid off. 'I grew out of a lot of my clothes,' he beamed. 'I went from a men's small to a men's large.'

Weitz confirmed the good news that followed, saying, 'I'm very happy that Taylor will be playing Jacob Black in *New Moon* and that he's doing so with the enthusiastic support of Summit, the producers and Stephenie Meyer.

'The characters in Stephenie's books go through extraordinary changes of circumstance and also appearance, so it is not surprising that there has been speculation about whether the same actor would portray a character who changes in so many surprising ways throughout the series. But it was my first instinct that Taylor was, is, and should be Jacob, and that the books would be best served by the actor who is emotionally right for the part.'

Taylor was understandably delighted with the news that he was to continue as Jacob, telling journalists, 'My experience on *Twilight* was wonderful and I am looking forward to continuing on with the team for *New Moon*. I have been working hard preparing for the physicality that this role will require and can't wait to get started with the filming of *New Moon*.'

Not only was Taylor delighted, but so were the cast members, who had already begun rehearsals for the second instalment in the series.

'I'm so glad they didn't have to find somebody else – we already had him,' said Kristen. 'I did not understand all the deliberation on whether to bring him back. But now that's its set, we can all rest.'

Nikki Reed beamed, 'I'm so proud of him. He didn't have the part. Everybody knew he was going to have to fight for this. He was at the gym twice or three times a day. He was on a nutrition and workout regime for the last year not knowing if he would be in this film.'

'We were all on edge. It got closer and closer, and it was heartbreaking. Kristen and I were in Africa when we got the call saying he got the part. She's so stoked.

'I don't know if I would have had the confidence to do that, and be told "no" if it didn't work out. He just went in there and said, "I'm going to do the best that I can." And it paid off. I'm so happy for him.'

Weitz would cast a little more light on his thinking about Jacob when the filming of *New Moon* was finished. 'The character in the second book is meant to be 6ft 5in, let alone transform into a werewolf and all that stuff. And Taylor, having only done three days of work in the first [film], it was time to take a pause and say, "Should Taylor go ahead and do it?"

'My overwhelming feeling was, "Yes, absolutely, let's go forward with it". To me, it wasn't a very difficult decision. For Taylor, it wasn't difficult at all. He knew the character, and he embodied the character – as people are going to see in the movie.

'So it wasn't really as tense and as scary a moment as it was portrayed in the media,' he added.

Talking to *Life Story*, Weitz added, 'I think he had such a small role in the first one and the studio really wanted to be absolutely certain that he was the right guy. I was certain from Moment One, and we all kind of came to that decision together. I never had any doubts at all.

'The fans have taken to him, because I think they

saw the same potential in him that I always did from the first movie. I think in the first film he didn't really get a chance to be the character that he was going to become, but people are going to be really surprised. His performance is really nuanced. I'm really pleased with how it's going.'

Through hard work, determination and talent, Taylor had managed to pick himself up from the setbacks of his TV series failing and the public debate about his future in *New Moon* and had transformed himself. Now the real test would start.

chapter seven

New Moon

'I think the fans would love anybody who played Jacob. I'm just lucky to be the one who got the chance.' – Taylor Lautner

The character of Jacob comes into his own in *New Moon*. But it nearly didn't happen like that. 'Originally, Jacob was just a device,' said Stephenie Meyer. 'Bella needed a way to find out the truth about Edward, and the conveniently located Quileute Tribe, with all their fantastic legends, provided a cool option for that revelation. And so Jacob was born – born to tell Bella about Edward's secret.

'Something happened then that I didn't expect. Jacob was my first experience with a character taking over – a minor character developing such roundness and life that I couldn't keep him locked inside a tiny role. From the very beginning, even when Jacob only appeared in chapter six of *Twilight*, he was so alive. I liked him – more than I should for such a small part. Bella liked him. Her instinctive trust and affection came without my intervention.'

Luckily for Jacob – and Taylor – Meyer's editor fell in love with the character as well, asking Meyer if they could get more Jacob in the story. Because Meyer was writing *New Moon* at the same time as she was polishing *Twilight*, she managed to go back and 'weave more Jacob through *Twilight* more centrally.'

As to whether Meyer's affection would lead her to choose Team Jacob over Team Edward, she is evidently torn. 'I can't choose a side. I love both characters so much, it's like choosing between my children. I'll admit I have a special place in my heart for the Jacob fans, just because they're so outnumbered.'

Taylor – who has, not surprisingly said, "I'm definitely Team Jacob!' – is now a huge fan of the books. 'I actually wasn't much of a book reader at all before the *Twilight* series. They just draw you in and people love them. They're terrific books. The series is great. I've never, never really read any books besides *Twilight*. Very rarely, maybe an occasional schoolbook. People are always like, "*Twilight*, is that that teenage chick flick book?" No, it is not.'

He proved his fan credentials when he gave Twilighters a big surprise at the release party for *Breaking Dawn*, Meyer's last book in the series, in Michigan. Taylor turned up to sign copies of the books, much to the joy of the excited fans. 'I was in my home town and thought it would be fun to go to the *Breaking Dawn* release party. I was there until 2am, hanging out and signing books. It was a good time. There were over a thousand fans there and it was a nice surprise for them.'

Taylor is as modest as ever about his own appeal, preferring to put fan attention down to Jacob's pulling power as a character. 'I think the fans would love anybody who played Jacob. I'm just lucky to be the one who got the chance.'

But in *New Moon* Taylor definitely gets to make his own mark. With Edward leaving, it's Jacob whom Bella seeks comfort in. However, getting the love triangle right proved tricky for the film's screenwriter, Melissa Rosenberg.

'I think we've found the balance, because the other thing you're doing is setting up another relationship, which will lead you into book three, which is a triangle and introduce the new addition. But I will say it's a challenge because you want Edward in there as much as you can. And what's true is that her entire storyline throughout the movie is really about him, there are other elements, but they're all motivated by having lost him or feeling the pain of having lost him. You have to keep that alive which actually ended up being not as difficult or as big a reach as I initially feared.'

With all the focus on female attention, director

Weitz is keen to highlight Jacob's appeal to male fans. 'I think that Jacob is probably more accessible to guys, because he's much more of a normal guy who works on cars and motorbikes and is relatively bumptious and friendly. Also he does convey that aspect of a person who is always there for someone and is a good guy.

'So is Edward in his own way, but much more dangerous and inaccessible. There's more of an action element and a CG element as well. I think, essentially guys are realising that if they don't go with their girlfriends, their girlfriends will leave thinking about Edward or Jacob – or they can be there with their girlfriends instead!'

It was a weird return to the franchise for Taylor. Not just because he had faced being replaced, but because when they first started filming they could never have believed how big the series would be.

'It's the weirdest thing. Nobody really saw it coming. I mean, we knew we were making a movie of a very popular book, but we didn't know how well it was going to do. When it opened, it exploded, and that was not something any of us saw coming. Filming *New Moon* is a lot different than the first one because this time we know what we are getting into. It puts a little more pressure on us than it did before. But for the most part, it's been a blast.'

There could have been trouble shortly before filming began when a script for *New Moon* was found in Missouri. Beauty salon owner Casey Ray found it – and another script called *Memoirs* (both Summit films and both starring Robert Pattinson) – in a litter bin outside an upmarket hotel in St Louis. It is thought that Anna Kendrick (who plays Jessica) had accidentally left them in her room while staying in the hotel. Luckily for the film's bosses, Cassey showed her good nature by giving the script back to the studio rather than cash in on her find.

A studio spokesperson said, 'We thank Ms Ray for doing the right thing. She has been promised premiere tickets for this gesture.'

Memoirs, incidentally, is a weepie drama, which has had a name change. It's now called *Remember Me*.

Perhaps there was something of a *Twilight* curse, because the fifth book in the series – *Midnight Sun*, which would have seen the story of the first book *Twilight* being told from the perspective of Edward – was shelved after the first few chapters were leaked onto the Internet, resulting in an upset Meyer claiming the book was over in a terse statement.

However, she has since said that the statement, which included the line 'If I wrote it now everybody would end up dying' – was 'kind of tongue in cheek'. And she has since spoken about working on it again.

'It's really complicated, because everyone now is in the driver's seat, where they can make judgment calls. "Well, I think this should happen, I think she should do this." I do not feel alone with the manuscript. And I cannot write when I don't feel alone. So my goal is to go for, like, I don't know, two years without ever hearing the words *Midnight Sun*. And once I'm pretty sure that everyone's forgotten about it, I think I'll be able to get to the place where I'm alone with it again. Then I'll be able to sneak in and work on it again.'

chapter eight

Transformations and Triangles

'There's double the action in this one.' Taylor Lautner

Straight away, Taylor found that working on *New Moon* was going to be much different from *Twilight*. Not only was he in it more, but he had to come to terms with how tough it can be to play a character who undergoes numerous changes, while having to shoot the movie out of sequence.

'He's a lot different than he was before,' Taylor explained. 'He transforms mid-story. In the first half, he's *Twilight* Jacob. I'm wearing a wig. My character's very clumsy, outgoing and friendly. When he transforms into a werewolf, he becomes something very different. It's like I'm playing a split personality. Which is tricky, because sometimes I've had to play pre- and post-transformation Jacob on the same day of filming.

'I think the most important thing with Jacob is that pre-transformation, he's clumsy. He trips over his own feet. As soon as he transforms, he's very agile. At one point, he flings himself through Bella's window and lands at her feet, and that's the first time Bella realises this is a new Jacob. He never used to be this agile. I loved bringing out that side of him. The bummer is, when he becomes a wolf, that's not actually me. When he does the cool fight scenes, he's transformed into CGI.

'I want them at the beginning of this film to see this really happy, nice, sweet guy that they fall in love with – and then all of a sudden POOF! He's a completely different guy and you cannot even believe it's the same dude.'

Of course the one thing that fans wanted to see was the famous love triangle, and Taylor promised that fans wouldn't be disappointed. '*Twilight* develops the relationship between Edward and Bella. In *New Moon*, Edward leaves and Bella needs someone to bring her out of this depression she's in, so she turns to her best friend, Jacob. It looks like it could go past friends. Bella's very confused. Jacob wants nothing more than to be more than friends. He wants Edward to get out of there so he can move in for the kill.

'Bella's torn. She's still in love with Edward, but she's kind of fallen for Jacob, too. When I read the books, I feel bad for Jacob, because he can't have what he wants. I understand Jacob's pain but also Bella's pain – how she's confused and torn between the two.'

If there were worries that the presence of a new director might unbalance the camaraderie between the cast members, they were soon erased. Jackson Rathbone, who plays Jasper, said, 'Whenever we got back to film *New Moon*, the first day I was back, the cast was hanging out in Peter Facinelli's room and it was just like a family reunion.

'It was like we'd been away for a month; it didn't seem like a year. It was just really nice to kind of get back together and have that family environment. In terms of having a new director, nothing really changed too much. It was just a different subtle vibe, because the director manages the energy on set. It was great. We all wanted to come together and make another great piece of art for the fans. It's really about what they want to see, because they're the ones buying the tickets.'

'The whole cast is really close,' Taylor confirmed. 'It would be difficult for our characters if we weren't. It's a love triangle, and we need to understand each other. So the fact that we're close and can talk things through in rehearsals, and if we're out at dinner, we'll just randomly start talking about the scene we're shooting the next day … If we weren't able to do those things, I don't know where we'd be.'

Taylor was also looking forward to working with

Chris Weitz, eager to pay him back for allowing him to return as Jacob. 'I've seen a few of his films, and he's really talented,' Taylor said. 'I mean, Catherine had a really interesting mind. [Weitz] has that as well. I've heard a lot of good stuff about him so I'm excited to meet him. I heard he's like a surfer dude, and that he's really laid back and friendly. It'll be fun.'

In *New Moon*, we finally see Taylor in action. It's ironic that he is a champion karate star yet he was the one of the few who hardly did any action in *Twilight*. Whereas he has won all these martial arts awards, it ended up being Robert Pattinson who was the action hero!

Pattinson said of his action scenes in *Twilight*, 'The wire stuff is quite fun when you're getting hit, but if you're trying to look like you're in control, it's really hard. It's actually exhausting, especially when you're trying to make it look easy. I'm not a stunt man at all. It's pretty tough. All of the action stuff was hard. The next movie I do, I want it to have no stunts, no makeup, no hair, no nothing.

'I'm really not an action movie kind of guy at all, and a lot of scenes were set up like kung fu movies. I've done wirework before, and trying to maintain your centre of gravity is tough and it can look really fake, really easily. And I didn't have that much time to practise. They took a pretty big risk, letting me do a lot of it.

'In the rehearsals, I was practising it when Kristen is holding on to me without a wire, and climbing up ladders and stuff. I was really fit at the beginning of the shoot and I lost all my fitness progressively. It seemed really easy when you're doing it at first. You're starting and there's something natural about it, and Kris only weighs like 50lbs or something. But it was terrifying as well. It was literally that high up on the edge of a cliff, and we had to climb up it with a very flimsy little rope. And it was freezing cold and it was wet. That part of it was just a miserable experience.'

Despite getting more of an action role in the sequel, Taylor can't show off his martial arts moves because the wolf aspect is special effects. However, Team Jacob were delighted to learn that David Slade – hired to direct the third instalment of *The Twilight Saga: Eclipse* – hinted that he was going to use Taylor's martial arts prowess for the movie. He posted a picture from the set of the film, which sees a shirtless Taylor in mid-air while executing a perfect back flip. 'Yes, that is him mid back flip,' Slade wrote. 'He does it from standing still.'

Taylor was not only back in but he was getting some friends too. They would be called the Taylor Lautner wolf pack. In a bid to ensure all the actors were from the Native American or First Nations community, they 'had to have papers that proved their heritage', said Weitz.

One of them is Kiowa Gordon. The actor, who starred in *Bandslam* alongside *High School Musical*'s Vanessa Hudgens, told MTV about the wolf pack.

'The head is Sam Uley – he's played by Chaske Spencer, who is a great guy. He's the leader of the pack; he runs us and helps us go through our phase. Next is Jared – he transforms next, and he's the fun boy, the jokester. He's played by Bronson Pelletier, and he's a funny guy too – he's awesome, we became really close. And Alex Meraz plays Paul – he's the hot-headed, ferocious guy that always wants to be in the middle of the action, and he's the go-to guy if Sam needs something taken care of.'

As Gordon was new to the series, he was stunned when the *New Moon* cast went to Comic Con in 2009. Experiencing the same feelings that Robert and Taylor had felt when they went there the year before, he couldn't believe the attention he received.

'It was crazy. They all started screaming as soon as we walked off the bus. The whole time we were answering questions they just kept screaming and screaming. It was so surreal for me. I've also gone to my own things – like I've gone to this unity conference out in New Mexico where Native

American youths gather and share their tribal affiliations and all that awesome stuff. And [Twilighters were there and] they went crazy.'

Other new cast members included child star Dakota Fanning and Michael Sheen. The latter plays Aro, the leader of an Italian vampire clan called the Volturi. 'Michael's role is so important because he's the head of all vampires,' Weitz said. 'I see this great British actor as being capable of anything. I was impressed when I saw him on stage playing David Frost as such a clever and manipulative character. I aggressively went after Michael.

'I think he's quite brilliant and conveys an extraordinary intelligence. Aro is, on the surface, a very gracious and friendly vampire, but beneath that he is a tremendous threat, which I think Michael Sheen can absolutely convey.'

Sheen is best known for playing Tony Blair in *The Queen* and David Frost in *Frost/Nixon* but he also played Lucian, leader of the werewolves, in the *Underworld* movies. 'I like to be able to jump around in that way,' Sheen said. 'It's an actor's dream to be able to play Blair one minute, Frost the next minute, and then lord of the werewolves the next.'

This time he plays a vampire leader, and Sheen noted, 'It's interesting that in searching for monsters to play, you often end up playing leaders.'

Fanning plays Jane, a member of the Volturi clan who has the ability to torture people with the illusion of pain. 'It's definitely different from anything I've ever played,' she said of her character, 'to get to play someone who's a little evil for once.'

She had spoken publicly about her hopes of getting the part before she officially signed on – a sign that she was a fan of the franchise. 'I haven't read all the books, but I've seen *Twilight* and I'm a very big fan of the cast. Pretty much all my friends are big fans, so it's been great.'

Talking about Fanning, Sheen said, 'I think Dakota may look the most unsettling. So angelic yet so weird. Like an evil Red Riding Hood.'

For Weitz, this was something of a second chance for him at adapting a fantasy franchise for the big screen. His first attempt – 2008's *The Golden Compass*, an adaptation of the first instalment of Philip Pullman's award-winning *His Dark Materials* series – wasn't the blockbuster that everyone had hoped for.

Despite its literary credentials, estimated $180 million budget and a cast including Nicole Kidman, Daniel Craig and Eva Green, the film failed to charm critics or cinemagoers. 'It's one of the great sadnesses of my life that it didn't turn out the way I intended it,' he would say later.

New Moon is famous for its love triangle. While many fans were committed to Team Edward after *Twilight*, you can now expect more Team Jacob fans. A lot of that was down to the moving and involving story by Meyer, but Taylor also helped the cause with his hunky new physique. His intense workout routine had had the desired results, attracting some attention from his cast mates.

'He's really buff,' beamed Kristen. 'He definitely is. If I had seen the Taylor who did *Twilight* and compared him right now with the one doing *New Moon*, he's an entirely different person physically. It took him so much time. He's so devoted.'

'It's insane!' Ashley Green gushed. 'I was going through my phone and looking at all the pictures, and there's one from the wrap party that we did here after the first one and it's incredible. I was like, "Taylor, did you see this?" He was like, "Oh my gosh." He gained 30lbs. He's not a little kid any more.'

And Christian Serratos, who plays Angela Weber in the movies, admits even she's torn to which team she should be in. 'I love the hoodies that say "vampires" and "werewolves," but I refuse to get one because I can't choose; I have to have them both. I have the Team Edward T-shirt, but I also have Team Jacob,' she revealed.

Weitz had told the wolf pack that they all had to be in good shape because a lot of their scenes would be topless. 'It's not pleasant for the actor, but they have all been good natured,' Weitz said. 'They show up on location in drenching, cold rain and I say, "OK, off with the robes."'

This made the wolf pack actors very competitive. Meraz said, 'We are pretty much half-naked the whole time, running around and lurking. We had to watch what we ate all the time, and before we started filming a scene we would all be on the side of the set with the dumbbells, lifting and curling and doing pull-ups.'

Spencer added, 'Between takes we'll do push-ups and they keep dumbbells on set. We're constantly working out. [The key] is muscle confusion – using the same muscles but with different routines. I've been eating six meals a day: fish, chicken, vegetables and protein shakes. It'll be nice to be a couch potato again.'

Even Weitz was shocked by Taylor's transformation. 'I think that Taylor is really going to surprise people in the movie. People have seen his body and all that stuff, and it's a shocker because it's hard to believe that anyone can be quite so carved. But he actually delivers a really great performance. He wasn't just exercising all day. He was also reading the book quite a lot.'

No matter how hard Taylor worked out or read up on the character's story, it would all hinge on what the werewolf looked like. Weitz, however, insisted his special effects team would more than deliver.

'I suppose one of the reasons that I got hired is that I have experience with these talking animals [during his time on *The Golden Compass*]. Actually, the werewolves don't talk in this, but I always felt they had to be CG werewolves – we couldn't have guys walking around in wolf-suits and we couldn't have animatronics. They had to be CG and they had to be just right. They had to be beautiful, they had to be elegant, they had to be perfect.

'These special effects take time to develop and to get through the pipeline, and you're editing and working on them throughout the entire process. To make them as good as possible and make them as integral to the story and to the characters and theme as possible within such a limited time is a real challenge.

'When they turn to werewolves in this story it happens very, very quickly. They're giant wolves basically. They behave like them, although they have sentience. That they acted like giant wolves was very important, that we not do anything hokey in that regard.

'So they're not really monsters in the traditional sense, and what's difficult about that is that now you have to make photo-realistic, non-stylised, giant wolves, which is tough, but we've got some of the best in the business doing it. I managed to get the band back together who did *The Golden Compass* and won the Oscar for the special effects to do this.'

By all accounts, Weitz was a calming presence on the set of the movie, despite all the hype and media expectation attached to the sequel.

'Catherine was a lot of fun, had a lot of energy,'

Taylor said. 'Chris is very calm and sees what's going on. Sometimes you just sit back and go, "How are things going *soo* well and *soo* smoothly while he's just *soo* calm?" I mean, he's such a great guy – he's really amazing and so talented it's ridiculous...'

Just as Taylor had to overcome difficulties with driving a car in *Twilight*, in *New Moon* he had to try and get to grips with Jacob's motorcycle. 'I've got mad skills,' he enthused. 'The dirt bike scenes are a lot of fun. I like a lot of the stunt stuff, so it's really cool to do that.'

He also has a tattoo in the film, but it's a special effect rather than the real thing. 'It's just like normal tattoos like you get from the 25-cent machine [but] it obviously works a little it more than 25 cent. Just stick the towel over the top and water – works pretty nice.'

But don't expect the muscled look to stay following the end of the series. 'When we're done with the *Twilight* films I'll definitely bulk down and just get lean again because I don't want to stay big and bulky.' However, he has pledged to keep bulking up for the remainder of the films. Talking during the MTV Movie Awards in the summer, he said, 'Jacob's character is continually growing throughout the series, so I've got about eight weeks off before I go back again for *Eclipse* and I'm going to be hitting the gym.'

Following Summit's decision to keep him in the

series, the Taylor who attended the following Comic Con in 2009 was a more confident and assured one. He was no longer the supporting character in the Edward and Bella show. He was one of the main players, reflected by his Best Male Fresh Face at the Teen Choice Awards.

Talking at the press conference, he joked with Stewart and Pattinson, with Kristen constantly holding Taylor's arm aloft to show off his muscles.

'It's exciting,' Taylor said. 'Last year Comic Con was an eye-opener for us so it's great to be back to embrace all of our fans again for everything they have done this past year.' He was certainly embraced by the fans, with Taylor revelling in his new role of being the centre of attention. As he showed off his new buff physique to delighted fans, it was almost a case of 'Robert who?'

Two scenes in particular stand out for Taylor in *New Moon*. 'My original favourite scene was this small scene which I thought was kind of cute. I walk her [Bella] to her door and say goodbye to her and I'm going off to fight in the woods and she's worried and scared for me. I thought that was cute.

'I also like the break-up scene.'

'That's my favourite scene too,' Kristen agreed. 'Well, we call it a break-up scene because essentially he tells me we can't be friends any more. And he's transforming.'

'It was very painful to shoot,' Taylor added. 'It was 35 degrees and it's pouring with film rain – ice cold. It was bad, really bad.'

But, Taylor promised, 'There's double the action in this one. There's also a new dynamic. Now there's not just a romance between a human girl and a vampire but it's the beginning of a love triangle.'

Kristen had her own opinion on the triangle. 'It's really very sad. It's a very typical girl thing to have this sort of ideal man in your life, and it's sort of a fight to stay with him. It's not easy. But you have your counterpart, like your best friend, standing right there who's the perfect option for you and who loves you and it's comfortable and it's easy.

'But you need more than that. So it's very masochistic. She's willing to ignore what is perfect for her, because she needs the fire she gets from Edward instead of the lukewarm comfort that she gets from Jacob, even though it would be so much easier and would live a much more comfortable life.'

While Weitz admitted that there would be less Edward Cullen in this film, he doesn't think the fans will mind too much – because Taylor is there to save the day. 'We wanted to avoid just randomly inserting Rob throughout the movie,' the director said. 'You'll see quite a lot of Rob in the film, but it's seen subjectively, through Bella's eyes. It's also in dreams that she has of him as well.

'It strikes this very fine balance between too much Rob and too little Rob... Well, I know for a lot of people there's no such thing as too much Rob. We've got a nice dose of Taylor to sweeten any Rob deficiencies. It is a disease that can only be treated with Vitamin T, for Taylor.'

chapter nine
Twilight
Pressures

'The only way to establish any kind of mystique is to completely shut up and never talk to anyone. And I'm contractually obligated not to shut up'
– Robert Pattinson

With Taylor no longer a supporting player and now very much one of the main team, he will no doubt experience the same sort of media attention and focus that has followed Robert Pattinson and Kristen Stewart around. The pair are constantly subjected to daily gossip, rumours and speculation. Paparazzi follow Robert and Kristen around to the extent that if Rob and Kristen forget where they are supposed to be filming that day, the paparazzi will be able to tell them.

Talking to *Dazed and Confused*, Kristen said, 'They just wait for you. It's insane. I went to the wrong place this morning and this person's like, "Hey Kristen, I think you're in the wrong place!"

'Normal 19-year-old people in this world f**k up

and make mistakes – they're late and almost get in car accidents all the time. It just happens and it's normal, they pull over into a parking lot. I can't back out of it, because it's crowded with people shouting things like – "Hey Kristen, you lost? Are you smoking pot? Are you f**king Robert Pattinson? You know, we have a call sheet, and you're supposed to be at the production office now."

'And that's when I'm like "Oh, my god! How in the hell do you have a call sheet?" A call sheet! I swear, if it's one of those guys in the office selling that shit, I will kill them.'

It's clear that Robert and Kristen have struggled to cope with all the fuss. But while Rob usually keeps his discomfort behind closed doors, Kristen will openly vent her displeasure.

'The fact is, the paparazzi and most interviewers, they want your soul. It's so scary because your persona – and I guess now I have one, because people think of me in a certain way – is all based entirely on quick snippets of crazed moments in your life. And that is what people then base their entire opinion of me on.

'Look, I love what I do and I know how lucky I am to be doing it. But I guard against being insincere, and I try not to say really cheesy things. I could say the whole "I am so grateful for this, I get to put my heart and soul into something everyday and people appreciate it…" blah, blah, blah. But to say something like that seems so trite to me – a cliché of an actress talking about acting. I don't talk like that, and so now people say, "Oh, she's ungrateful, she's a bitch."'

Kristen shot to fame in 2002's *Panic Room* alongside Jodie Foster and has worked with some of the biggest names in Hollywood, including Sean Penn, Robert DeNiro and Sharon Stone. But she's always struggling with the adverse side effects that fame brings. She hated going back to school after *Panic Room* because of the abuse she received from her classmates. 'People would scream at me. Kids are mean,' she recalled.

'Anywhere we'd go for *Twilight* was a psychotic situation,' she added. 'The sound was deafening, and it's thoughtless, as well. You get a slew of all these bullshit questions like, "What's it like to kiss a vampire?" and "How much do you love Robert?"'

'I was getting really paranoid,' Rob added. 'But then I realised that if tomorrow I say, "OK, I've had enough, we're stopping everything," it won't change anything. Might as well try to accept it and stay zen, as I have no control over it. It's not always easy. But whining won't change anything.'

Taylor, however, has a different attitude to fame. His family made sure he was aware of the burgeoning media attention. 'My friends and family send me links to fan web sites. It's pretty cool,' he said. So when Robert and Kristen experienced the huge crowds at 2008's Comic Con in San Diego, it was Taylor that they turned to.

'Both Rob and Kristen have come up to me and asked, "How do you not freak out? What do you do?" And they're all sweating. I tell them, "I don't know. I mean, this is fun!" But they're all disappointed, like "Oh, OK."'

But with the focus more and more on Taylor, he's starting to see the other side of fame. While it's great to experience the occasional rush of attention like a premiere or a big event like Comic Con, it's adifferent entirely when it becomes a daily thing.

'There are 12 cars that camp outside my house,' he told MTV in 2009. 'You can't ever really get used to it, because it's not normal to have people snapping pictures of everything you do. You just have to try not to let it affect you.'

As for the fans, Taylor said, 'They are very intense, but it's cool that they're so dedicated and so passionate. They're the reason we're here doing this sequel. So I'm thankful for the fans. I like meeting them. But, yeah, they're pretty intense. Sometimes it becomes a little overwhelming.

'We've met many different fans: the criers, who come around quite often; the hyperventilators who stop breathing and have to have a medic come. We've definitely seen some passion.'

It's lucky then that the cast get on so well. They are a close-knit bunch who have seen their stock rise from either unknowns or promising actors to superstardom. And they have managed to get through it by sticking together no matter what, as shown by the way they publicly spoke out for Taylor when it looked like he might miss out on *New Moon*.

Taylor is thankful for their support, but he also has his family to keep him grounded and his many sporting pastimes to keep him busy. He still hangs out with his friends from school, saying, 'Kids still looked at me as Taylor, because they knew me from before. You gotta remember who your friends were before you got famous.'

His dad, Dan, added, 'We had no idea what was gonna happen. We tell him, "You have no idea what's gonna happen tomorrow, so enjoy today. Have fun."'

But if the attention ever gets too much for Taylor, he just needs reminding about why he made these films in the first place.

'Sometimes it gets me nervous because I'm trying to live up to people's expectations. I'm trying to represent Team Jacob in the right way. I don't want to disappoint them – that's why I worked so hard in a way to mentally, emotionally and physically change for this role. Because [Rob] is pretty good competition!'

chapter ten

Taylor the Heartbreaker

'I'm a teenage boy, so I date.' – Taylor Lautner

It's not only Robert Pattinson who has made the headlines with romantic rumours. Taylor has had his fair share of speculation as well.

One girl he has been linked to is *Zoey 101* actress Victoria Justice. They were snapped in Vancouver while he was filming *New Moon*. However, Justice insisted she wasn't dating Taylor. 'We became good friends while auditioning for *Sharkboy and Lavagirl*,' she explained.

Not that Taylor is in a rush to find love. Apart from a two-year relationship with his former classmate Sarah, not much is known about his love life. 'I don't have one in particular, but I have had a few important girls over the years,' he told the *LA Times*.

'I don't think I really know how to flirt,' he added in another interview. 'I'm not out there or creepy like some guys are. I'll take my time and make sure everything is good, and that I really like the girl.'

One girl it seems he does really like is teen actress Selena Gomez, who has dated Nick Jonas in the past. Gomez had tongues wagging after she and Taylor were often spotted together. Even more tellingly, she has been seen with Taylor's parents and his sister.

'I think she's so cute and I think he's so cute,' said Ashley Greene of the friendship. 'They should date.'

'He's one of my good friends,' Gomez said. 'Kristen was staying in my hotel. Taylor would visit her, so we were constantly running into each other in the lobby – and we ended up meeting. We would go out to lunch and dinner, but I knew he had paparazzi following him and I had paparazzi following me,' she explained.

'So we literally just wanted to hang out, go bowling and stuff, and it went a little too far, I think. People were getting a little crazy about us... but it was fun. I went to Vancouver thinking I was going to focus on my work, but instead I got to meet him, and it ended up being the best thing ever.

'He is so sweet. Taylor has made me so happy. I didn't know I could be that happy... He's a great guy but I'm 100 per cent single and I'm going to keep it that way for a while.'

If anything, Gomez is in the Team Edward camp after watching *Twilight*. 'I can totally see the Robert Pattinson thing now, that's for sure!'

Taylor was also linked to actress Ashley Tisdale, but she soon scotched that one. 'No, I'm not dating Taylor Lautner,' she said. 'I have a boyfriend. No idea where that got started.'

In one of the more bizarre rumours involving the *Twilight* cast, it was claimed that Pattinson was becoming jealous of Stewart and Taylor's budding relationship. Rob, who has been frequently linked with Stewart despite their many denials – was said to have expressed his concern with the pair.

'Taylor definitely has a crush on Kristen,' a source told *Star* magazine. 'She treats him like a little brother.' The source added that Taylor's many presents for Kristen was a particular annoyance. 'He looks for rare, vintage things, which he knows Kristen likes.'

Taylor has branded the love triangle rumours 'crazy'.

It was clear, however, that Kristen and Taylor had grown close through filming *New Moon* – largely due their attempting to replicate the chemistry in *New Moon* that Kristen and Pattinson had had for *Twilight*.

'It was vital,' Taylor said. 'Edward and Bella's relationship is so intense, but Jacob and Bella's is very laid-back.'

Kristen admitted that their real life relationship is 'lamely cute' – a description which is fairly apt for Bella and Jacob's relationship.

'Sometimes there's a question of, "Is it going to go past best friends?"' Taylor continued. 'And sometimes it looks like it. But they are so open, and they can tell each other everything. So it was very important for me and Kristen to grow very close before doing this. It wasn't like we went out to, like, theme parks together or anything. It was just, like, going to each other's houses, hanging out, going and getting some dinner. A lot of nothing – just spending time together.'

Taylor was also incredibly grateful for Stewart's support when there were rumours that he might be replaced for *New Moon*.

'It's completely understandable why they wanted to make sure he was right,' Kristen told *Entertainment Weekly*. 'He was so young, 16, so I got it. But I knew he had it. Just because of how I felt around him. I literally saw Jacob in him.

'I love that kid,' she added. 'I would do anything for him. I would kill for him, literally.'

So Taylor is very much single, and he hasn't ruled out a fan!

'I think one of the most asked questions is "Would I ever date a fan?" Well, this is an easy one. I don't look at people as fan, star or celebrity. When I look at a girl, they have to have the things that are important to me and it does not matter what they do or how well known they are. How well known they are does not matter to me at all.'

chapter eleven

Eclipse

'I'm excited to get going.' – Taylor Lautner

Because of the huge success of *Twilight*, Summit decided to make the next two films back to back – with a view to releasing them just under a year apart. For that reason it would have been impossible for Weitz to direct the third one. While the cameras would be rolling on *Eclipse*, he would have to be editing *New Moon*. And just as with *New Moon*, there would be plenty of drama before the cameras on *Eclipse* would roll.

Firstly, there was the fuss over who would direct it. Some unusual names were mentioned – including former child star Drew Barrymore. 'I'm one of the directors that is being talked about, which is great because I'm a director now,' she confirmed. The former wild child's directorial debut was the high school comedy *Whip It!* which stars *Juno*'s Ellen Page.

Another name mooted was Spanish director Juan Antonio Bayona, who earned rave reviews for 2008 horror tale *The Orphanage*.

Talking about the directorial choices, Kristen Stewart urged, 'As long as they get someone who's invested, as long as they get someone who cares. It's so above me, but I think that both are good choice in their own way. I'm sure that they'd be great. Drew's been doing this her whole life, and she's pretty cool.'

In fact, it ended up not going to either choice: David Slade was hired to direct the third instalment of the *Twilight* series. Slade is no stranger to vampires after his impressive directing turn on the truly scary *30 Days of Night*. There were no vegetarian vampires in that film, though – it was a very full-on action film.

Stephenie Meyer said, 'I am thrilled that David Slade will be directing *Eclipse*. He's a visionary filmmaker who has so much to offer this franchise. From the beginning, we've been blessed with wonderful directorial talent for the *Twilight* saga, and I'm so happy that *Eclipse* will be carrying on with that tradition.'

Summit's Erik Feig said, 'Stephenie Meyer's *Eclipse* is a muscular, rich, vivid book, and we at Summit looked long and hard for a director who could do it justice. We believe we have found that talent in David Slade, a director who has been able to create complex, visually arresting worlds. We cannot wait to see the *Eclipse* he brings to life and brings to the fans eagerly awaiting its arrival.'

Slade didn't get off to the best start, however, when *Twilight* fans learned that he once tweeted that he would prefer to be shot than to watch *Twilight*. He was left red faced when he was offered the chance to direct the third film shortly after his comments.

To rectify the matter, he said, 'When I made these comments, I had neither seen the film nor read the books. I was promoting a comedy short film that I had made for Xbox and every pop culture subject matter was seen as a possible comedy target. I was being silly and none of the statements were from the heart.

'Of course, I have seen the movie and read the books and was quickly consumed with the rich storytelling and the beautifully honest characters that Stephenie Meyer created. I would like to reassure everyone involved that I am invested in making the best film that I am humanely capable of, and that I am acutely aware of the power of the original books we serve.'

Slade also responded to concerns that his two films – the brutal revenge paedophile thriller *Hard Candy* and the aforementioned *30 Days of Night* – didn't showcase a director who can handle the more romantic elements of the franchise.

'Even though people think I'm a really violent and unpleasant person, I actually do have this romantic-violent side to me.'

Producer Wyck Godfrey maintained that they had made the right choice. 'Ever since I saw *Hard Candy*, I was obsessed with him as a filmmaker,' he said. 'That's a female point-of-view movie, and it's very different than the average female point-of-view movie. He's also done tons of videos that are female friendly, and he has some teeth to him too, which I think is good.'

Peter Facinelli added, 'I've heard he's very intense, and I heard he's a great actor's director, so I'm excited to work with him.'

This time there would be no worries for Taylor over whether he was to stay in the series. This was particularly great news for him as *Eclipse* was his favourite book in the series. 'I like that. It's got action. The action keeps building so I enjoy that.

'The first relationship is between Bella and Edward, while Jacob gets to build his relationship with her in *New Moon*, but in *Eclipse* we all come to a decision to try and team up to protect her, so that is the ultimate high point of the series for me – the love triangle. So I'm excited to get going on that.'

Talking about the triangle, screenwriter Melissa Rosenberg noted, 'The third book is about the triangle, and this is the episode where Bella chooses between Edward and Jacob. She's chosen when we start the movie but then she has to go through a process of elimination. She starts by choosing from a teenage, immature place – "That's what I want" – but then she really has to look at that choice, because everything and everyone is forcing her to look at that choice, and has to make that choice from a very mature place and [by] really looking at the consequence of this choice.

'The whole movie is really about choice and consequences, and I think that requires some very delicate handling. You're talking about some very subtle emotions and you really have to track that, and it comes to looking at both these guys as a viable option.

'And in looking at both lifestyles and what they offer as options – it's really about "Who am I and who am I going to be? What do I want for my life?" It's a very mature question to ask, so finding that answer will require some exploration.'

Summit again toyed with the idea of replacing a main character – and this time the studio decided to wield the axe. Rachelle Lefevre, who had played Victoria thus far, was dropped because of scheduling conflicts – that was the official reason anyway.

Lefevre, however, hit back at the suggestion that her involvement on the low-budget film *Barney's Version* alongside Paul Giamatti was the reason for her exit. 'I was stunned by Summit's decision to recast the role of Victoria for *Eclipse*. I was fully committed to the *Twilight* saga, and to the portrayal of Victoria. I turned down several other film opportunities and, in accordance with my contractual rights, accepted only roles that would involve very short shooting schedules.

'My commitment to *Barney's Version* is only ten days. Summit picked up my option for *Eclipse*. Although the production schedule for *Eclipse* is over three months long, Summit said they had a conflict during those ten days and would not accommodate me. Given the length of filming for *Eclipse*, never did I fathom I would lose the role over a 10-day overlap.

'I was happy with my contract with Summit,' she added, 'and was fully prepared to continue to honour it. Summit chose simply to recast the part. I am greatly saddened that I will not get to complete my portrayal of Victoria for the *Twilight* audience. This is a story, a theatrical journey and a character that I truly love and about which I am very passionate. I will be forever grateful to the fans' support and loyalty I've received since being cast for this role, and I am hurt deeply by Summit's surprising decision to move on without me. I wish the cast and crew of *Eclipse* only the very best.'

Summit Entertainment responded with their own version of events. 'We at Summit Entertainment are disappointed by Rachelle Lefevre's recent comments, which attempt to make her career choices the fault of the Studio. Her decision to discuss her version of the scheduling challenges publicly has forced the studio to set the record straight and correct the facts.

'Ms Lefevre's representatives were advised as early as April that *Eclipse* was expected to start shooting in early August. If Ms Lefevre was, as she describes, "passionate", about being part of *The Twilight Saga*, we feel that she and her representatives would have included us in her decision to work on another film that would conflict with the shooting schedule of *Eclipse*.

'It was not until 20 July that Summit was first informed of Ms Lefevre's commitment to *Barney's Version*, a commitment we have since been advised she accepted in early June. Summit had acted in good faith that she would be available to fulfill her obligations both in terms of rehearsals and shooting availability for *Eclipse*. We feel that her choice to withhold her scheduling conflict information from us can be viewed as a lack of cooperative spirit, which affected the entire production.

'Furthermore Ms Lefevre took a role in the other film that places her in Europe during the required rehearsal time, and at least ten days of *Eclipse*'s principal photography. This period is essential for both rehearsal time with the cast and for filming at key locations that are only available during the initial part of production.

'Contrary to Ms Lefevre's statement, it is simply untrue that the Studio dismissed her over a ten-day overlap. It is not about a ten-day overlap, but instead about the fact that *Eclipse* is an ensemble production that has to accommodate the schedules of numerous actors while respecting the established creative vision of the filmmaker and most importantly the story.

'The fact remains that Ms Lefevre's commitment to the other project – which she chose to withhold from Summit until the last possible moment – makes her unfortunately unavailable to perform the role of Victoria in *Eclipse*.'

Rumours then began to circulate that her exit was because of financial reasons. A source told *E! Online*, 'Summit could have made it work. But they saw that they could save a lot of money by recasting her. This could get really messy.'

Lefevre was also a popular member of the young cast. 'They'd all come and talk to her about everything,' the source added. 'She knew all the drama on and off set.'

Victoria was now to be played by another actress, *Terminator: Salvation*'s Bryce Dallas Howard. Summit's Erik Feig confirmed the news, saying, 'We are incredibly happy that Bryce has agreed to come into the franchise. Rachelle brought Victoria to great screen life and Bryce will bring a new dimension to the character. The franchise is lucky to have such a talented actress as Bryce coming in to fill the role.'

The story took another twist when *Twilight* director Catherine Hardwicke revealed that Howard had actually been the first choice for Victoria. Talking to *LA Times*, she said, 'I know we originally asked Bryce Dallas Howard to do the first movie but she thought it was too small a part at that time.

'I cast [Rachelle] so I wish they could have worked out something. I wasn't involved in the negotiations so I don't really know the inside story... Either of them would have been good.'

The film itself sees Bella again in danger as she is forced to choose between her strong feelings for both Edward and Jacob, knowing that her decision could trigger a war between werewolves and vampires. For Team Jacob fans, *New Moon* gives Taylor much more screen time – and the chance to prove that the producers made the perfect choice.

chapter twelve

The Future

'I love the Bourne series and I wouldn't mind doing something like that.' – Taylor Lautner

Some actors would rest on their laurels after being catapulted to stardom by the *Twilight* films. Not Taylor. The young actor is determined to be a major Hollywood star, and with his track record of his karate career, his long-haul commutes for auditions and coming through the whole *New Moon* casting saga, it's clear that when Taylor has his heart set on something you wouldn't bet against him achieving his dreams.

Talking to *Vanity Fair*, he said, 'I'd love to do a movie with Denzel Washington, or some action star such as Matt Damon or Mark Wahlberg would be really cool too. I love the Bourne series and I wouldn't mind doing something like that.'

He's also a big fan of Tom Cruise. Talking to

ultimatedisney.com, he said, 'One of my favourite movies is *The Last Samurai*. I love that movie. I guess I kind of like it because I can relate to it. I started out with the traditional Japanese martial arts and then I went into the extreme new modern version.

'In that movie, they started out with the Samurai and the traditional fighting in war, and then they go to the more modern one. So I guess I could relate to it well and it just got me really in the moment. I thought that Tom Cruise did a great job portraying that role.'

And don't be surprised if you see Taylor featuring in a superhero movie, as he's a huge fan of that genre too. 'I love watching the *Spider-Man* movies. Although he's probably not [my] favourite superhero, I love watching the movies. As for a superpower, I like X-Ray vision, like Superman, who can see right through things. I think that's pretty cool.'

Could we be seeing Taylor play the Caped Crusader's sidekick Robin in the next Batman movie? He's certainly got the martial arts skill for the role.

Taylor will next be seen in romantic comedy *Valentine's Day*, which follows the adventures of a series of different couples and single people coping with the highs and lows of the romantic holiday. The movie is a who's who of Hollywood's finest, including Julia Roberts, Shirley MacLaine, Jessica

Alba, Ashton Kutcher, Anne Hathaway, Jessica Biel, Jennifer Garner and Jamie Foxx. It also sees Taylor getting into a clinch with US singing star Taylor Swift.

Remarkably, *Valentine's Day*, Taylor's first post-*Twilight* film, is scheduled to be released in the USA on 12 February 2010 – the same day as Robert Pattinson's big solo outing, the drama *Remember Me*. So is there going to be a box office battle between Team Edward and Team Jacob? Whichever team you're on, you can be sure both actors will be making massive waves in Hollywood in the future.

vampire VS werewolf

blood | rivals

Robert Pattinson
The Biography

vampire vs werewolf

blood|rivals

Robert Pattinson
The Biography

JB
JOHN BLAKE

Published by John Blake Publishing Ltd,
3 Bramber Court, 2 Bramber Road,
London W14 9PB, England

www.johnblakepublishing.co.uk

First published in paperback in 2009

ISBN: 978 1 84454 916 0

British Library Cataloguing-in-Publication Data:

A catalogue record for this book is available from the British Library.

Design by www.envydesign.co.uk

Printed in Great Britain by CPI Bookmarque, Croydon, CR0 4TD

3 5 7 9 10 8 6 4 2

Front cover images and internal photographs reproduced with kind
permission of Rex Features and Getty Images.

Papers used by John Blake Publishing are natural, recyclable products made
from wood grown in sustainable forests. The manufacturing processes
conform to the environmental regulations of the country of origin.

Every attempt has been made to contact the relevant copyright-holders,
but some were unobtainable. We would be grateful if the appropriate
people could contact us.

To Nia, for all her help and support

Contents

Introduction

The Twilight Saga is the classic tale of a love triangle that has divided the nation. Who should Bella Swan choose? The dashing, mysterious and undead Edward Cullen? Or the loyal, besotted and shapeshifting Jacob Black? The endless debate for *Twilight* fans rages on.

But now, it's more than that. The rivals are no longer confined to the pages of a book, but have exploded onto the scene as two of the biggest upcoming Hollywood stars of the moment: Robert Pattinson and Taylor Lautner. For millions of fans around the world, Robert Pattinson *is* Edward Cullen. And for them, there is only one side: Team Edward.

Since you've flicked onto the Robert Pattinson side of this book, you're obviously a big fan of the

tousled-hair actor. And you'll be pleased to hear that Robert's portrayal of the brooding and angst-ridden Edward Cullen isn't that far off his off-camera personality as well (apart from the vampire aspect, obviously!).

Robert is a dynamic, passionate and single-minded individual – and is someone who has strove to find his place in the world by doing it his way and no one else's.

Welcome to his story.

Prologue

The date was 3 December 2007. It was a cold winter day in London, but if you were anywhere near the city's Leicester Square you couldn't fail to notice the temperature rising. The reason for that was a certain young actor who was about to step out of the cold into the heated atmosphere of the UK premiere of *Twilight* – a story about a young teenage girl who falls in love with a vampire.

After his car had pulled into position, his feet had barely touched the black carpet (replacing the customary red one) when the whole square shuddered with a cascade of screaming noise and flashing lights. The sound was deafening, the atmosphere electric, and standing slap-bang in the middle of it all was a clearly dazed and startled Robert Pattinson.

The 21-year-old actor was there to promote a film with his 18-year-old co-star Kristen Stewart, but it was clear that the majority of the fans were there for the handsome young British actor. 'He's one of us!' screamed one of the hundreds of girls who had braved the freezing cold to catch a glimpse of their new idol.

'It's absolutely mad,' said the actor, stumbling for words as his brain began to process the attention he was receiving. He then made his way into the cinema, the screaming cheers still ringing in his ears.

Inside, the place was packed with celebrities and a who's who of film industry and media people, all desperate to see what the fuss was about. The lights went down and the film began. And then it happened: Robert's character Edward Cullen made his dramatic appearance – strutting in slow motion with the camera lingering on him – triggering audible gasps from female members of the audience. Instantly, the question in everyone's minds was, 'Who is this Robert Pattinson and how on earth did he become such an overnight star?'

Except, of course; his success hadn't come overnight. Robert's career has had more twists than his trademark tousled hair. The story of how a sensitive young man, who had shied away from mainstream Hollywood in favour of quirky independent dramas, ended up starring in one the biggest film series of modern times, is an eventful and fascinating one.

Childhood

'He was sweet, cute and quite quiet.' – Robert's aunt

Robert Thomas Pattinson was born in London on 13 May 1986 at a private hospital in Barnes, the same area where he would enjoy a loving and happy childhood with his parents Clare and Richard, and his two older sisters Elizabeth and Victoria. Barnes is an affluent riverside suburb, with the many elegant and luxurious 19th-century buildings proof of its high-end reputation.

'My dad is from Yorkshire and he did a bunch of things,' said Rob. 'In the 1970s he moved to America for a bit and just worked as a taxi driver. Then he started selling cars in the 1980s. My mum worked as a booker at a modelling agency and now they're both retired.' Typically, Robert was playing down the fact that his dad had actually

forged a lucrative business importing vintage cars from America.

Robert was brought up with a strong work ethic instilled in him from a young age. While his parents were well off financially, he and his two sisters were never spoilt, with their parents ensuring that they knew the value of money by chipping in every now and then.

'I started doing a paper round when I was about 10. I started earning £10 a week, and then I was obsessed with earning money until I was 15,' said Robert. He still hasn't forgotten his values, buying not a fancy sports vehicle after landing the *Twilight* job but a second-hand car.

Clare and Richard also ensured that their children were well educated in politics and the arts. 'I used to get very passionate about politics,' Robert remembered, 'but I don't know enough any more. My dad is very, very political and his whole deal is to always take the opposite argument to the person he's with, even if he doesn't agree with it. I spent my whole life dealing with that, and so you had to be really up on all your stuff.'

In an alternative world, Rob could have been more famous for his politics than his acting, because he briefly considered taking it up for a career. 'I didn't achieve much, but politics was what I wanted to do while I was in school, yeah. I just liked the whole idea of it. I wanted to be involved with politics.

That's what my whole plan was, I was going to go to university and then I just thought, "Ah, I can't be bothered to do anything. I don't want to do any more homework."'

He now concedes that he struggles to be up-to-date with current affairs because of both the time factor and the fact he's now in the showbiz world, but jokingly quips, 'I know all about Miley Cyrus!'

Rob grew up in a household of warmth and laughter. 'Rob got his quirky sense of humour from his father,' recalled his Aunt Diana Nutley, who told *Us* magazine, 'They are a very close-knit, middle-class family. He was brought up very modestly.'

Richard and London-born Clare met in a pub in Surrey through a mutual friend when she was 26 and he 35 – and the pair had quickly agreed on the way they would raise their three children. They would let them choose their own path, but there was one thing they did insist on.

'My mum, sisters and I speak really well,' Robert explained. 'My parents were just aware of how you're treated differently in the world if you speak articulately. So it was just the way I was brought up.'

As was humility, it seems. One of the things that Robert is praised about is his lack of ego, despite his big success with the *Harry Potter* and *Twilight* movies. He's never been one to overshadow his other co-stars, preferring to let them bask in the limelight. An appearance in 2009's Comic Con in San Diego

was testament to that, with Robert refusing to do a solo interview and insisting it had to be with fellow cast members Kristen Stewart and Taylor Lautner, who play Bella Swan and Jacob Black in the series.

'He was sweet, cute and quite quiet,' remembers Diana Nutley of her young nephew. Indeed, while most actors and music stars generally regale the media with stories about their childhood that usually involve being the centre of attention at family gatherings or rehearsing their future Oscar speeches to a mirror, Robert was an insular and thoughtful child. True, he was also playful and could be relied on to provide wicked witty deliveries, but they were only done around his small, trusted circle of friends.

'There's just very few people who I think are worth the time,' he said. 'I don't like talking on the phone; I can't really maintain relationships with people who don't want to come hang out with me. Most of the time I feel like I'm wasting my time anyway, so instead of hanging out with people, I'd prefer to create something rather than go out and talk with someone.'

His desire to be in a small, loyal group, be it with his school friends or cast mates, rather than go through life meeting a constant stream of brief acquaintances is testament to the close bond with his family – not that living with two older girls didn't have its drawbacks.

He may be R-Pattz to his loyal legion of fans, but to his sisters he would always be called 'Claudia'. The girls were always trying to give their young brother a feminine makeover – hence the name. 'I was 12, my sisters used to dress me up as a girl and introduce me as Claudia!' explained Robert.

He also went by another nickname – Patty. Robert actually cherished the affectionate moniker and even, years later, named his pet dog Patty.

chapter two

Rob At School

'I don't like people telling me what to do.' – Robert Pattinson

Although the media describe Robert's upbringing as 'arty', he doesn't look back on his education at two posh private schools with fond memories. From 1992 to 1998, he attended Tower House School, a prep school for boys in nearby Sheen. Past pupils include the British actor Tom Hardy, who went on to star in the critically acclaimed movie *Bronson* in 2009. Robert then went to the independent, fee-paying Harrodian School in Richmond, again not far from home, which was co-educational.

Even at a young age, the roguish Pattinson was very happy to be attending a mixed school. 'Twelve was a turning point, as I moved to a mixed school, and then I became cool and discovered hair gel,' he

said, with a twinkle in his eye. Twelve was also the age at which Robert had his first kiss.

It should come as no surprise that Robert was popular with the opposite sex – his looks won him an army of admirers long before his face featured on many a bedroom wall. 'He was an absolutely lovely boy,' said Tower House School secretary Caroline Booth. 'Everyone adored him. We have lots of lovely boys here but he was something special. He was very pretty, beautiful and blonde.'

Couple his looks with his almost rebellious and poetic persona during his later school years and it was no surprise that he became something of a heartthrob. However, Robert is quick to quash that reputation, insisting that he wasn't very much of a rebel. 'I was quite shy,' he has said of his schoolboy self.

His Aunt Diana remembers that he 'had lots of friends, but he didn't date much.'

Both schools are establishments that pride themselves on academic excellence, with Harrodian telling its students that 'good manners and consideration for others are expected, and European and global awareness promoted.' The school's mandate also states that its aim is that 'children should be encouraged to reach their fullest potential – academically, physically and socially – in a happy atmosphere. In particular, children are taught to be articulate in English and confident in French.'

But it was a rigid and strict environment that wasn't best suited to Rob's outlook on life. As for being confident in French, Rob said, 'I speak French, sort of. At, like, a three-year-old's standard.' Instead he seemed more suited to soaking up art and culture than academic learning.

'My favourite teacher was probably my English teacher, because she got me into writing instead of just answering the question. I used to hand in homework with 20 pages of nonsense and she'd still mark it. She was a really amazing teacher.'

She obviously still inspires him, as Robert is attempting to add another string to his bow – he wants to be a successful author. 'I have been trying to write a book. It's a novel, but it is kind of a strange novel. It's kind of sci-fi, but not really sci-fi. I have been trying to write it for ages and ages.'

The other classes didn't do it for the young Rob, but another aspect of his character may have had something to do with that. 'He was hopelessly lazy,' his Aunt Diana remembered. 'He didn't really study very hard.'

'I wasn't very academic,' Robert admitted. 'My school reports were always pretty bad. I never ever did homework. I always turned up for lessons as I liked my teachers, but my report said I didn't try very hard.'

When Robert did take his studies seriously, he normally excelled himself, but those times were few

and far between. He admits that he only really tried when his like-minded friends would all compete with each other when something took their fancy.

'The few times that we decided to do homework we'd just be competing with each other. If it was an English essay or something, we wouldn't do 90 per cent of the homework, and then something would come along with an interesting title and we'd all do, like, a thesis on it just to beat each other. I've kind of grown up around really competitive, artistic type people, luckily, and I'm very, very grateful for that as well,' he told US magazine *Life Story*.

His schoolmate Will Robinson remembers, 'Rob had a very, very big grin on his face constantly and was cheeky in class. Everyone liked him.'

It wasn't that Robert was an unruly student – although he did win the Untidy Desk Award in 1998 – nor was he mischievous. It was just that he preferred to daydream in class rather than study. 'I like looking out of the window. I'm pretty relaxed most of the time.'

Despite his indifference to the education system he ended up being a lunch monitor at Harrodian, but it was a role that he never took seriously. 'I used to take everyone's chips,' he joked.

Considering that fees at Harrodian were just over £4,000 a term, it is understandable that his dad was having concerns about Rob staying at the school. 'If I got into trouble at school, I made sure I was playing

the piano when my dad got home from work, and then he wouldn't be able to tear me up.'

However, according to Robert, his dad did finally tell his son: 'OK, you might as well leave, since you're not working very hard.'

Rob's other aunt, Monica Weller, carried on with the story: 'His dad said he'd have to pay his own fees, then he'd pay him back if he got good grades. So Rob modelled to pay for school. And he got an A and two Bs. Rob has got good values and a strong work ethic.'

'His career has evolved very quickly – he was in the right place at the right time. We're all hugely proud of him.'

Looking back now, Robert concedes that he should have concentrated harder at school. 'I wasn't focused on school and I didn't achieve much. I remember that now, and I always try to remind myself not to waste a moment of life. If I could have done one thing differently, I think it would have been that I would have taken school more seriously.'

As his Aunt Monica said, Robert did modelling while he was at school. If his first job was delivering newspapers and magazines, his next one saw him appearing in them. Given his mother's knowledge of the modelling industry, some might have thought she would pull favours to get him a job, but Robert's striking looks and easy-going charisma were always likely to get him noticed. He soon

landed a series of jobs, including photo shoots for teen magazines.

'I was modelling at 12, the youngest person in my agency out of the girls or boys,' Robert said. 'I was so ridiculously skinny I looked like a girl, but that was the period when they loved androgynous-looking people.

'Then, I guess, I became too much of a guy, so I never got any more jobs. I had the most unsuccessful modelling career.'

He added, 'I always get referred to as an ex-model, and I maybe did three jobs. I did, like, women's ring modelling. I used to do it in catalogues 'cause I have very feminine hands. Still do.'

Rob later fell back into modelling, appearing in men's clothing company Hackett's autumn 2007 campaign. His film career was going to be much more successful and fulfilling, but that was still a long way away. He hadn't really been bitten by the acting bug yet, but just as he felt he was coming to a crossroads in life, fate, or more accurately, a group of good-looking girls, stepped in.

A Thirst For Acting

'I owe everything to Barnes.' – Robert Pattinson

'Robert has wanted to be an actor for as long as I can remember,' Robert's Aunt Monica remembers, but Robert's move into acting came as the result of something completely unexpected. 'My dad was in a restaurant and saw a bunch of pretty girls,' he said, 'and he decided to go up to them and ask them where they'd been. They said they went to this drama club and he says, "Rob, you've got to go down to this club."

'That's the only time he's done anything like that. It was just the weirdest thing, and he had nagged me about attending. At one point he said he would pay me, which is pretty strange. I don't know what his intentions were.'

Robert's intentions weren't perhaps entirely

honourable themselves. Explaining why he went there, he smiled, 'Lots of pretty girls went there.'

Both Tower House and Harrodian schools had excellent drama facilities. The former states that their drama club will help students 'gain invaluable experience in performing in front of people in a relaxed, uninhibited environment' – while Harrodian boasts 'first rate drama productions, art exhibitions and musical events'.

Tower House secretary Caroline Booth remembers, 'I wouldn't say he was a star but he was very keen on our drama club, I do remember that.

'Robert wasn't a particularly academic child but he always loved drama,' she told the *Evening Standard*. 'We're all so pleased that he's found something he really shines at.'

Despite these first-rate facilities and an early part, when Robert was six, in a play called *Spell for a Rhyme* (written by a Tower House teacher) and a role as Robert in William Golding's *Lord of the Flies*, it was the Barnes Theatre Company that helped develop the young man into the actor that he has become.

At this stage in his life, though, Robert was becoming less and less secure in himself. 'I was shy, withdrawn and I didn't have any self-esteem,' he once said. 'The year that I was 17 was one of the worst of my life, because I was searching for my place in the world.'

In an intimate interview with *GQ* magazine, he said, 'I was constantly thinking that I was faking my emotions. I was constantly attacking myself: "You're a fake, you're a fraud."

'I remember when I was a teenager thinking my girlfriend was cheating on me, and going around riling myself up. Pretending to cry. It was totally illegitimate – I actually didn't feel anything. I went to some pub and then went crying all the way home. And I got into my dog's bed. I was crying and holding on to the dog. I woke up in the morning, and the dog was looking at me like, "You're a fake."'

It turned out that the girl in question wasn't even cheating on him! 'I thought I'd seen her with another guy, but she wasn't there. I spent three days apologising to the dog.'

So it's perhaps understandable why his dad was so keen to persuade his restless son to join an acting group. It was a chance for him to obtain some confidence, meet new people and maybe, just maybe, develop some skills at this acting lark. So, following his dad's encounter with that group of girls, Rob joined the Barnes Theatre Company amateur group.

'It was a drama school right around the corner,' recalled Robert. 'I had never done any acting before. I really wasn't part of the acting fraternity at my school, but I ended up joining this thing after my dad argued with me for ages. I went there and worked backstage for a while.

'I never really did acting at school or anything. I was quite shy throughout my life, so I never really considered it.'

Despite working backstage for a while, it was clear that Robert was meant to be in front of the stage curtain, not behind it. 'I just decided that I should try to act, so I auditioned for *Guys & Dolls* and got a little tiny part.'

What Robert learned straightaway was the pure release he got when performing. While some go into their shell when having to perform, some latch onto the experience with relish. He was very much the latter, even at this early stage.

'I liked having something to work up to and then having the nerves and everything,' he said. 'I like performance; it's the same with music. You can kind of get disorientated and lost when you're on stage, much more so than you can in reality. Being disorientated and lost in reality is not a very pleasurable experience, but if it's on stage, it's kind of controlled.'

While he was to find that acting was a great antidote to his low self-esteem, he also discovered that he was a natural on the stage. To Robert's surprise, the performance gene runs very much in the family. 'My dad recently said to me, "I really am an artistic person." I was shocked, as I never saw him as creative. I think me and my sister [Elizabeth] are living out that side of him though, as my sister is another creative person. She's a songwriter.'

While it was a small step for Rob into the acting world, he would take a bigger leap in the next theatre production – American playwright Thornton Wilder's *Our Town* – by bagging the lead part.

'I wasn't an "actory" kid or anything,' Rob said. 'I didn't do drama in school. I went to this drama club when I was about 15 or 16 specifically because a girl, who I really liked, went there and that was it. I worked backstage. I never had any intention to do it and then they did *Guys & Dolls*. I really wanted to play the Nathan Detroit part so much – just completely out of the blue. I have never sung in public or anything. I just suddenly got obsessed with it. I did the audition and didn't get it. I played the Cuban dancer instead.

'Then all the good people left. For the next production, it was Thornton Wilder's *Our Town*. I was the only one tall enough to play the lead. I did that.'

Robert wasn't to know it but Lady Luck was smiling down on him. Some actors go through years trying to get their break, but he got his almost instantly. While Robert was plucking up the nerve to step out in front of an audience for the first time as a leading man, what he didn't realise was that there was an agent at the play. Luckily for Robert, she was suitably impressed by his performance. It may have not been note-perfect but she could see that this was a raw and vibrant talent.

'I did a play,' Robert recalled, 'an amateur drama

club, and the guy who ran it, his daughter was an agent and she watched the play I was doing. It was actually the first play I'd ever done in my whole life and I got an agent from that. It was just complete luck. I'd never thought about it. I'd never given the tiniest bit of thought to being an actor.'

So Robert got an agent, but he never did get the girl who was the reason he kept turning up at the theatre group. 'No, I didn't. She thought I was nuts when I told her after, so it didn't really work out. But she was the reason I actually started acting. She was the girl who I went to the drama club for.'

Summing up the whole experience, Robert said, 'So many people from there had become actors. Rusty and Anne, who are the directors, were actors themselves and were very talented. They were a very good group.

'I wouldn't be acting if it wasn't for Barnes Theatre Club. I owe everything to that little club. In a weird sort of way, that stuff was probably the best I've done and the stuff that I am most proud of.'

Barnes gave him a taste for acting, and it's one that he has never given up on.

'You watch something like *One Flew Over the Cuckoo's Nest*, and you leave the cinema and your walk has changed. It gives you a kind of confidence just watching something that really rubs off on you. I like being able to create something in a movie, in acting, where you can

actually be how you would want to be. It's the only way you can really concentrate on something.'

'Plus,' he added cheekily, 'you get to shoot guns and stuff!'

From that he went on to bag a role in a stage production of William Shakespeare's *Macbeth* for the Old Sorting Office – an arts charitable trust based in Barnes, which helps nurture young acting talents. They put on several productions, as well as giving budding actors professional advice to help improve their craft.

'He's had no professional training,' Rob's aunt Monica said. 'He wasn't a member of RADA [Royal Academy of Dramatic Art] or anything. It's all from amateur dramatics. We're all very proud of him.'

chapter four

Robert's Magical Role

'Cedric is competitive, but he's also a nice guy who plays fair and sticks to the rules.' – Robert Pattinson

Robert was learning his craft and improving with every role that he was given, so he must have thought he had landed his big break when he bagged a role in the 2004 movie *Vanity Fair*. Directed by Mira Nair, the film is an adaptation of the 19th-century social satire by the novelist William Makepeace Thackeray. It stars Reese Witherspoon as a poor young woman called Becky Sharp, who attempts to climb all the way up the social ladder.

Summing up the whole unlikely scenario, Robert said, 'My first job: I was Reese Witherspoon's son and I hadn't done any acting in school. I wasn't in a drama school or anything. I'd done one amateur play and end up doing a film with Reese Witherspoon.'

Despite his brief turn in the film, the Oscar-

winning actress remembered her time with him. 'I remember he was verrrrrry handsome! I was like, "I have a really handsome son!" I had to sob and cry all over him, but he was great.'

But Robert's joy turned to sadness when he found out that his brief scenes were axed from the final cut – although they can now be seen in the deleted scenes section of the *Vanity Fair* DVD.

It must have come as a huge shock for Robert. o Perhaps it stood him in good stead, because when he did get his break in later years, he kept his feet on the ground. He would not have taken it for granted after suffering the devastating and embarrassing blow of his performance being excised from this movie.

One suggestion for his performance being cut is that he looked too old to play Witherspoon's son – she was only ten years older than him. It was an opinion that Rob shared. 'She was 27 at the time and it was ridiculous.'

Despite the crushing disappointment, Robert can now look back on the whole confusing experience with something resembling fond memories. 'You have a trailer and stuff. It was the most ridiculous thing. And I was thinking, "I shouldn't be an actor. I'm doing a movie with Reese Witherspoon. How is this happening?"'

Robert loved the freeing, creative and generally unrestrained aspects of acting. It was a world away

from humdrum 9–5 day jobs at the office. 'It's the one job where you can do whatever you want and people have got to accept it. If you were going to an office, got upset, and said, "I need to go to punch out some windows because I have to do this database," you'd get fired. But you get a lot of slack as an actor, [so] you can just go nuts all the time.'

Not long after *Vanity Fair*, Rob was given another chance to make his mark on the movie world. He signed on to star in the 2004 fantasy *Ring of the Nibelungs*, which was based on a 13th-century epic German poem that had influenced JRR Tolkein's *Lord of the Rings*. But this was more than just a chance for the young actor to prove himself. Because the film was shot in Africa, Robert was to stay there by himself. For an independent free spirit like Robert, it was a once in a lifetime opportunity.

Unfortunately, the shoot coincided with his final school exams, so he had to juggle a demanding study timetable with his strict filming schedule. He still managed to achieve an A and two Bs, but Robert wasn't impressed with his academic performance. 'I don't know how that happened. I didn't even know half the syllabus. I lost faith in the exam system at that point,' he said.

Ring of the Nibelungs starred *Terminator 3: Rise of the Machine*'s Kristanna Loken, *The Exorcist*'s Max von Sydow and well-known TV actor Julian Sands, with Rob playing the role of a young

medieval peasant. The film received modest reviews, and there were some scathing ones – most notably, 'A teutonic Tolkien cash in, light on brains, brawn and budget.' But there the Tolkein comparisons stop, as *Ring of the Nibelungs* was light years away from the success of that blockbuster epic.

The movie went on to have a convoluted life, with several name changes and different versions being released. It had a limited theatrical release in some countries, went straight to DVD in others, while in Germany it was re-cut as a mini-series and proved to be a huge success. It has since become something of a curio item for Robert Pattinson fans – and a collection of his scenes have popped up on YouTube.

But things were about to get better for Robert, because his big break was just around the corner. He signed on to play Cedric Diggory in the fourth *Harry Potter* film – the most successful franchise in cinema history. And here *Vanity Fair* turned out to have been a blessing after all.

'I had just finished filming a role in Cape Town, South Africa,' Robert recalled. 'I was there for three months in an apartment at just 17, so I came back really confident. The casting agent on *Vanity Fair* was the same as the one on *Harry Potter*, and I was the first person to be seen for any part on the film, which could have helped.

In a bid to win the part of the sporty Cedric Diggory, Robert pretended he was fan of football

and snowboarding. In fact he prefers darts to playing football. 'I am not determined to do really weird parts,' he said, 'but I think I overdo it in auditions, so nobody really trusts me.'

The same could be said for the way he acts on set sometimes. Robert sometimes sees on-set camaraderie as distracting and something that could be viewed as not taking the film seriously enough.

'I didn't know how I would be interpreted so I went into *Harry Potter* determined to seem like a real actor and did not speak to anyone for a while. I didn't notice the transition to being accepted, but they are all really nice people. It seems like it should have been daunting, but it wasn't. We did a bonding week where we made fools of ourselves doing lots of improvising. I paired up with Rupert [Grint] a lot.'

Robert would take this same desire and intensity to the set of *Twilight*. He believed that the way to achieve the otherworldly feeling that Edward didn't belong was to make sure he didn't get too close to the cast. Speaking to *Moviehole.net*, he said, 'I didn't talk to any of the cast about anything other than the film for at least a month and a half of the shoot. It creates a strange aura around you, and people don't really know what to make of you. I just wanted the rest of the cast to think about me as a character being this intense person.'

Back on *Harry Potter and the Goblet of Fire*, Robert was determined to soak up the collective

acting experience on set. So he was delighted to be in a movie starring some of the greatest acting talents in Britain, including Sir Michael Gambon, Timothy Spall, Jason Isaacs, Dame Maggie Smith, Alan Rickman and Ralph Fiennes. 'They make it look so easy,' he raved. 'I mean, you watch and think "I could do that." They can do a lot of stuff in *one* take.'

Robert still laughs at his brief screen time with Ralph Fiennes, who plays Potter's nemesis Lord Voldemort in the series. 'I didn't really talk to Ralph Fiennes while I was doing *Harry Potter* and the only thing I did with him was when he stepped on my head! Then I went to this play and he was there, and this girl said, "You've worked with Ralph Fiennes, haven't you?" and I was like "Well, no..." and Ralph said, "Yes, I stepped on your head." And that was the extent of our conversation!'

Only one actor had Robert star struck, and it's probably not one you would have imagined. Warwick Davis, who stands at just under 4ft tall, plays Professor Filius Flitwick – but his most famous role is probably the title character in George Lucas' 1988 fantasy *Willow*. It just happened to be one of Robert's favourite films. 'I had one scene sitting next to him at the dragon's task,' he laughs, 'and I had no idea what to say to him at all. He was the only person I asked for an autograph the whole way through.'

It turns out that in his youth Robert was something of a sci-fi and fantasy fan. 'I sort of consider myself something of a geek. I went to a few sci-fi conventions in England, like *Doctor Who* ones, and I always found them really interesting. I guess I was a geek, but I was more a computer-game geek.'

Robert's interest in the subject hadn't extended as far as the *Harry Potter* books, however. Talking to the BBC after winning the casting, he said, 'I hadn't read any of the books or seen the films so I can't say I was a fan. I knew of them, it's impossible not to know about them. When I found out about the audition I read the book in about a day and knew I wanted to do it. There's something very special about it. I think people will be watching the films for years – there's nothing else like it.'

Robert was in awe of his new surroundings: nothing he had done before could compare to this. 'Since I started acting it's kind of been a bit mad. I never really did anything before and two years ago I started acting and I've kind of been in work ever since. Then *Harry Potter* came along and it's been a huge step and a massive event in my life.

'Things like special effects are probably one of the strangest things to go into if you have never done acting before. I did a lot of special effects in my last film [*Ring of the Nibelungs*] so it kind of helped, but on a smaller scale. The scale of *Harry Potter* is huge:

people have been working on it for four or five years. There are two thousand people working on the set – not many films can afford that kind of "epic-ness."' Robert admitted to being so anxious at the start of shooting that he would throw up because of the nerves. 'At first I felt a bit of pressure but after a week, when all the cast were known and they are all so nice, then the feeling was gone. When I was shooting my first scene, the maze scene, there was a crew of about 150 people, me, Dan [Radcliffe] and the producer. Later on, it became about two thousand people involved in shooting. I'm really glad I could get started in a more relaxed environment and get used to it progressively.'

Cedric Diggory is first mentioned in *Harry Potter and the Prisoner of Azkaban* before he makes his dramatic first appearance in *Goblet of Fire*. Talking about his character, Robert said, 'Cedric is competitive, but he's also a nice guy who plays fair and sticks to the rules. I sort of identify with Cedric in a couple of ways. I am not as nice as he is, he tends to do the right thing all the time and I never feel the need to do that. I think he's a pretty cool character.

'He's not really a complete cliché of the good kid in school. He's just quiet. He is actually just a genuinely good person, but he doesn't make a big deal about it or anything. He's just like, "Whatever." I can kind of relate to that. He's not an unattractive character at all and his storyline is a nice storyline to play.'

Daniel Radcliffe, who plays Harry Potter, said of Robert's character, 'He's the archetypal hero who gets the girl – and in this case, my girl. But Cedric and Harry ultimately bond through mutual respect and a combined sense of fair play.'

Director Mike Newell explained, 'Cedric exemplifies all that you would expect the Hogwarts champion to be. Robert Pattinson was born to play the role – he's quintessentially English with chiselled, public-school boy good looks.'

The movie turned out to be a really long shoot. 'It was kind of tiring by the end,' Robert admitted. 'I was on it for about 11 months or something. But all in all, it was really fun, and there were a lot of amazing times, which was really nice.'

As Robert said, it was a tough shoot for the young actors. One scene in particular saw him and Radcliffe having to film a gruelling underwater sequence. 'There was a lot of underwater stuff, which I quite liked,' recalled Robert. 'It felt therapeutic after a while. I had never scuba dived before and the tank they taught us in was a little bathtub. The real thing was massive and they expect you to just get in and act.

'It was really strange. It's completely blue in there and there are divers with breathing equipment that are completely blue as well. You can't really see anything. You just get this breather put into your mouth after the take has been done.

'We would do a 30-second take and I couldn't let bubbles come out of my mouth or anything, because I am supposed to be able to breathe under water in the movie.'

Talking about his character's dramatic death, Robert laughs, 'I looked at the other actors and thought, "God! Lucky you! You've got another three films guaranteed."' He did come back in a cameo flashback sequence in *Order of the Phoenix*, but his time in the franchise was essentially over.

But if Robert thought working on a huge film like *Harry Potter and the Goblet of Fire* was something to get used to, he was given another shock when he turned up at the London premiere. While he could take in the screaming crowd knowing that they were mainly there for Daniel Radcliffe and company, he was still incredibly warmly received. He would gaze at the screaming fans and wonder what it must be like to have that sort of attention all the time. It wouldn't be long before he learned what that would be like and then some, but at this point in his career he was just a cog in a very well-oiled machine.

'I was in a trance the whole day through the premiere,' he recalled. 'The day before I was just sitting in Leicester Square, happily being ignored by everyone. Then, suddenly, strangers are screaming your name. Amazing.'

But at least he could observe how the young *Harry Potter* actors coped with fame. 'No one's ever really

given me any advice. I mean, I don't really ask for it. But I guess just seeing how the *Harry Potter* people have dealt with it, and they're still very, very normal and sane.

'I think it's just because they ignored the surrealness of their lives from an outside perspective and just dealt with everything as complete reality. They just live their lives normally and don't treat anyone differently, including themselves. And they've ended up completely fine. I think there's no reason to change, really, that much. I mean the only reason to change if you want to be an actor is if you're completely insane and you don't want anyone to find out.'

While most actors would love to be in a film that had such a lavish premiere, Robert was different. Not only did the crowd stun him, but he also discovered that he hated watching himself on screen. 'I have never watched anything of myself since *Harry Potter*. I went to it because my whole family was coming to see it. Nothing comes other than this pure discomfort. I can't watch myself. I am just feeling everybody else's reaction. I can't handle that at all.

'It seems pointless watching it. You get a big ego or you become depressed. So I avoid it altogether.'

Although they went their separate ways, the *Harry Potter* actors are delighted about Robert's success. Daniel Radcliffe said, 'I won't pretend we're best

mates or knew each other really well but we really enjoyed working with each other, or at least I enjoyed working with him! He's doing brilliantly, which is fantastic.

'The thing that is interesting for me is that *Twilight* is the only other franchise that comes close to *Potter* in terms of the mania that surrounds it, the attention that the leads get and just how global it is.'
Tom Felton, who plays Draco, said shortly before *Twilight's* release, 'It's just great to see someone who has been in *Harry Potter* have a life after it, and a much bigger one! So I wish him all the success and I will see *Twilight* soon, I promise!'

Following the success of *Harry Potter*, Robert was briefly treated as the hot new thing in the British press. The London *Evening Standard* called him the 'new Jude Law', and shortly before the film's release he featured in *The Times'* 'Almost Famous' section, which looked at the most promising British acting talent around. They said the 'fresh faced, photogenic 18-year-old so oozes charm and likeability that casting directors are predicting a big future.'

If people thought Robert would be immediately thrust into stardom, they would be greatly mistaken. But Robert believes that the quieter period between *Harry Potter* and *Twilight* helped to keep him grounded following the huge media interest. 'Having been the hot thing for a few months and it just going and no one caring, it helps once you get used to it, to

know that no one will care. Once you're immune to failure, it's like nothing matters.

'What surprised me is how quickly the recognition switched from *Harry Potter* to *Twilight*. It's funny, because teenage girls would say, "Oh my God, you're Cedric." It switched to "Oh my God, you're Edward." Allegiances change so freely in the teen girl world.'

One thing *Harry Potter* did, however, was hammer the final nail in the coffin for Robert's other keen interest – politics. 'I was going to do the conventional thing and go to university to study International Relations. I wanted to be a politician but *Harry Potter* made that decision for me.

'I was always intending to go to university. But *Harry Potter* went into overtime, so I didn't have to think about going to university. I just fell into acting and then after I'd finished that movie, I was like, "Oh well, I guess I'm an actor now."'

chapter five

Crossroads

'I didn't know if I wanted to be an actor.' – Robert Pattinson

Following his breakout performance in *Harry Potter and the Goblet of Fire*, it seemed the new heartthrob had the world in his hands. However, when everyone expected Robert to go one way, he went the other. Rather than cement his status as The Next Big Thing by appearing in a soulless blockbuster, he preferred to make leftfield choices that would improve his acting talents rather than his bank balance.

'I wanted to try theatre after *Harry Potter* and I wanted to do something weird. I was offered an American thing where I had to sign up to three movie contracts and I dunno... I don't really know what I should be doing yet, so I prefer to do nothing really! There was one script that I really, really liked.

I got down to the last two and they picked the other guy, which was a bit annoying.'

Renting a 'cool little ex-crack den' in Soho, Rob and his childhood pal Tom Sturridge – another actor – would spend their time relaxing and playing music. It was a period that Robert describes as 'the best time I ever had.'

'We spent the better part of a year just getting drunk every night. [The flat] was so cool. You had to walk through a restaurant kitchen to get up to the roofs, but you could walk along all the roofs. I didn't do anything for a year; I just sat on the roof and played music.'

Sturridge, who had appeared in *Vanity Fair* as well, also featured on *The Times'* 'Almost Famous' list, with the newspaper reporting that 'he has grown into a young man with romantic lead potential'. In fact, the pair regularly competed with each other at auditions early in their careers. 'We go up against each other every single time, even though we look completely different,' said Robert.

When Robert did land himself another job, it was not something associated with a rising star. He signed on to appear in an obscure German play called *The Woman Before* at London's Royal Court theatre, alongside *Friends* actress Helen Baxendale. Robert was expected to star in it, but was replaced by Tom Riley shortly before the opening night.

'At the time I really thought "Wow, I must be great

– I'm like f**king [Marlon] Brando,"' Robert recalled later. 'I had this specific idea where "I'm going to be a weirdo, this is how I'm going to promote myself" and then of course I ended up getting fired.'

Clearly reassessing his situation, he told interviewers, '[Acting has] come along by accident. I've never trained or anything, so I've only very recently become even vaguely comfortable with it. On *Harry Potter* I was so conscious of the fact that I didn't know what I was doing, I used to sit on the side of the set throwing up. I think I will go to drama school now, though. I did a play which I got fired from in the West End and I realised I needed to learn some of the fundamentals – like how to act!'

Robert has since become more bullish about his exit from the play, telling *You Magazine*, 'I liked the freedom and in the things you could do with acting. Like if you want to look sad, you don't have to have a sad face, which is still how I try on a lot of different things. For that same reason – trying to take risks – I got fired from that play. I haven't really changed since I got fired.

'It's probably one of the best things that ever happened to me. I got some jobs afterwards by saying I got fired for standing up for what I believe in.'

Robert soon got another chance following the disappointment of the play, and grasped it with

both hands. He starred in the gripping British TV movie *The Haunted Airman*, based on the novel *The Haunting of Toby Jugg* by Dennis Wheatley. Robert played the titular character, a flight lieutenant who moves to a remote Welsh mansion after being wounded during World War II. Things take a turn for the worse when he begins to suffer terrifying visions.

'I play a pilot who gets shot and paralysed. He gets terrible shell shock and basically goes insane. It's a great part. I was in a wheelchair all the time, which is always good, just chain-smoking throughout the entire film.'

The Haunted Airman also gave him a chance to team up once more with Julian Sands, who had starred in *Ring of the Nibelungs*. Sands plays the creepy psychiatrist who examines him.

The Stage magazine described the film as 'a disturbing, beautifully made and satisfyingly chilling ghost story.' Robert was singled out for praise, with his performance earning rave reviews for his 'perfect combination of youthful terror and world weary cynicism'. There was inevitably a reference to his looks too – 'An actor whose jawline is so finely chiselled it could split granite!'

Next Robert starred alongside Catherine Tate in another British TV movie – a comedy-drama called *The Bad Mother's Handbook*, based on a novel by Kat Long. In it Robert plays a nerdy student who has

a crush on the daughter of Tate's character. It showed the usually dramatic actor in a more comedic light, highlighting his versatile talents.

Next up was the charming and quirky *How to Be*. First-time director Oliver Irving recalled Robert's audition. 'Robert walked into the audition and reminded me of people I know. I think he forgot his lines and just started improvising, which is exactly what I wanted – someone who could just become the character and leave the kind of techniques they train in at drama schools. I had a hunch he would do well with [the] other cast.

'He's a really down-to-earth guy. It was funny because he told us he had a part in a *Harry Potter*, but as you can imagine, many actors in England have had tiny parts in those films. Plus, he really underplayed it, so I didn't think much of it at the time. It wasn't until we had cast him that I watched the *Harry Potter* film he was in and realised he has a major part.'

Despite becoming a seemingly permanent fixture at independent film festivals across the world, *How to Be* struggled to get a distribution deal. 'It's very random,' Robert said, 'and that's why I liked it. It's almost impossible to market and when you see how they've tried to market it, you say, "That's not what it is."'

The film tells the story of a loner called Art – a struggling singer-songwriter who is battling to cope

with life's hardships. After his girlfriend dumps him, he goes on to move back home – with quirky consequences. It was a film and role that Robert fell in love instantly with.

'He's kind of ... I guess you'd call him a mediocrity. He doesn't really seem to fit into any kind of people grouping. He's not particularly depressed but he thinks he is. He doesn't have a consistency in his emotions, which is how I think most people are like. He's just basically chasing his tail. He's a guy who's really stuck in a rut. Art really feels like he can't break out of anything, that he's been trapped in his own life, and he's kind of resentful of that as well.

'He's a very demanding friend. He doesn't specifically ask for any thing, but he's just very emotionally draining for his friends. I guess that's why his friends in the movie are quite closed down to him, even though he seems relatively normal and sympathetic.'

To achieve the look for the character, Irving ordered Robert to do two things. 'I said, "You're banned from cutting your hair between now and the shoot." We had to give him the most awkward haircut we possibly could, and we cut his trouser length a little bit too high. Things like that played down his apparent good looks.'

How to Be came at a time when Robert was becoming disillusioned with acting. 'He was

thinking about giving up acting and maybe doing music solely when this role came along,' Irving recalled. 'He wanted to play the roles he wasn't getting. He was looking for something more challenging. [This] got him back into the swing of things again.'

It's a film that Robert looks back on fondly, and he's glad that it's reaped the benefits of his success. '*Twilight* is helping. I went to the Austin festival [for *How to Be*] and it was packed because of *Twilight*. I loved the script. I loved the ending. No one claps and he doesn't even notice. I thought that was such a feelgood ending, even though it's not really.'

Irving was obviously grateful for Robert's newly found A-list status. 'I've been really touched by the strong, positive response to this film. It's been amazing, the support we've had. When it first screened it did have a really good response. What has changed is the number of people in the audience. Some people have seen it several times as well, so members of the audience are really starting to be familiar with the characters and even coining catchphrases in some instances, which is great. I love hearing the laughter during the film, I really do – it makes it all worth it.

'Every so often someone will love the movie and never have even really heard of Rob,' he added. 'But then often people will say "I came because of Rob but I loved this film in its own right." I can tell from

what they say that their response is really genuine, so I am just glad that Rob's star factor has brought in potential audiences. I'm glad the film won the Grand Jury Honourable Mention at Slamdance [an annual independent film festival in Utah] long before Rob's stardom flared up. That eases my neuroticism somewhat.'

Other honours the film has won at festivals over the world include Best Picture prize and Best Actor for Robert at the Strasbourg International film festival and at the First Glance Film Festival in Hollywood.

The film was also a personal triumph for Robert, mainly because he could really relate to the character. 'It's just kind of feeling you don't really know where you're going in the world. At the time I thought that I didn't know if I wanted to be an actor. I didn't know what I was doing. I hadn't been to university.

'I was bumming around, not feeling particularly good at anything but at the same time desperately wanting to and thinking, "You'll never reach your own goals you set for yourself."'

Rob is delighted the film has had a kiss of life but it also served to underline his views that the movie industry doesn't give enough films like this a chance. 'I don't like the way the film industry is. If you come with a good script and then it goes to the studios and gets financing, it all gets changed because they want to make money. It's like, how do you know if

it's going to make money or not? All you're doing is making it generic when you do that, and making it generic is no guarantee that it's going to make money either.'

chapter six

Robert Gets Serious

'I didn't want to get stuck in pretty, public school roles.' – Robert Pattinson

The hype that surrounded Robert following the success of *Harry Potter* was soon forgotten. His résumé since then consisted of getting fired from a West End play and a handful of quirky roles. Robert was becoming more and more disillusioned with acting – not by the amount of roles he was being offered but by the quality. Too often they didn't match the standard he wanted – and when they did, they either struggled to obtain distribution or were dumped straight into the TV schedule. Even worse, some could take years to come to fruition because of the challenges of trying to raise finance for a movie.

But still Robert stuck to his ideals. As much as the ambitious young man wanted to a make a splash in the world of acting, he was keen to ensure that it was

on his own terms. Luckily for him, he got a chance to do just that after signing on to star in *Little Ashes* – a biopic of the famous artist Salvador Dalí. It was one of those projects that Robert had been circling around a long time, and he was delighted that he was finally given the nod to play Dalí.

Born in 1904, Salvador Domingo Felipe Jacinto Dalí is seen as the most famous artist of the Surrealist era. But it was his younger years, when he met the poet and dramatist Federico García Lorca, that would be the main focus of the film.

Director Paul Morrison said of the film, '*Little Ashes* is first and foremost a love story, moving and tender. This is a forbidden love between two men that moves from a silent, aching longing to an incandescent and glorious moment of promise, only to end in rejection and disillusionment. Lorca's love for Dalí gives the movie its shape, its dramatic spine. This is first and foremost an actor's movie, truthful and beautiful, intimate and spare. The performances dominate.'

In the film's production notes, he promised, 'The audience, with Lorca, will fall in love with the shy and brilliant Dalí, and be captivated by his sensitivity and vulnerability, hidden behind his poses and charades. We admire and fear for him in his outrageousness. Later, we fear more for Lorca as we realise that Dalí's masks have become his face, that he has begun to believe in his act, and that Lorca and

his love are becoming the victims of Dalí's narcissism and ambition.'

The lead part of Dalí was a great opportunity for Robert. But in the beginning, he was going to play the other lead part – that of Lorca, the homosexual poet who embarked on a passionate relationship with Dalí.

'For Lorca and Dalí, I must have seen every up-and-coming young actor who was available in both Spain and the UK,' Morrison said. 'Originally, Rob read for Lorca, and I was going to cast Dalí in Spain. But Rob felt so much more a Dalí – the combination of acute intelligence and vulnerability and self-consciousness that the part demanded – that I switched, and brought him back to read for Dalí. He was perfect. I never saw anyone in Spain who felt right for Dalí, by the way.'

'I was attached to that for about, I guess, two years,' Robert added. 'It took ages to get this film made. It was a really interesting script, and about a year after I was in mind for Lorca I read for Dalí, and about a year after that they suddenly said, "Oh, we've got money, we're doing it in Spain and it starts in four days!" So I came and just thought it would be kind of fun. I mean, you know the stuff Dalí makes – kind of crazy, and I thought it would be quite fun to do.'

But while it would be an incredibly satisfying job for Robert, it wasn't fun. 'I wanted to have

a vacation in Spain,' he said. 'But it became just – really, really hard. I'd never done a job that was so hard.'

While the logistics of shooting in an environment where most of the crew spoke a language that he didn't know were tough, the biggest sources of hardship were due to Robert himself. Typically, he didn't make things easy for himself. Determined to immerse himself fully in the role, he pored through hours and hours of research, trawling through the many contradictions that surround the playful and complex Dalí in a bid to find a true voice for the role.

'I couldn't speak to anyone the whole time. I just sat over this Dalí stuff. I just read and read and read, and it was one of the most satisfying jobs I've ever done because it was the one time that I really had zero distractions. It really changed my whole attitude towards acting. It was a tiny, tiny film, which I don't think anyone will ever see, probably. But it was very interesting, especially since I don't look anything like Dalí. But at the end of the job I kind of did look like him.

'When he was younger, if you read his auto-biographical stuff, he wrote three autobiographies which completely contradict each other. Literally in one of them he said that his mother sucked his d**k and all this stuff. And then in another one he says that his mother was the greatest mother in the whole world

and gave him the best childhood he'd ever had. There are chapters called Truth and the other ones are called Lies…. It's just really funny. There was so much about that that I found fascinating. He was an incredibly complex person.

'I wasn't even really that big a fan of Dalí's art. And even now, I kind of love the guy as a *person*. I mean, I find him fascinating, and in a really weird way I related to him a lot. And I appreciated the art a lot more. As with a lot of artists who are painters and stuff, I enjoy their art more once I know the back-story behind it.

'He was afraid of people knowing who he was. That's something I can really relate to as well. He was an incredibly complex person,' he said, quickly adding, 'I'm not saying that I am. I'm not at all.'

Although *Little Ashes* might look like the perfect film to counterbalance the mainstream success of *Twilight* and Edward Cullen, it was filmed before the blockbuster, despite being released after it.

However, Robert did notice that there were parallels between the two lead characters. '[*Little Ashes*] is a devastating love story. Two people fall in love but they don't know the extent of their relations and it ruins their lives, especially Dalí's, because he's such a sensitive man. In *Twilight* it's the same thing, but they figure it out.'

Later he would say to *Life Story* magazine, 'I don't think a lot of people are going to be thinking, "Wow,

this is exactly the same as *Twilight*." I think it's a little bit too different to have that happen.'

But one thing that is similar is that Robert is playing a character known to millions, even if one is fictional and one very real. Talking about how he approaches playing someone that audiences already have an image of in their head, he said, 'I think in a lot of ways it's kind of the same. If you're just judging anyone you're still playing fiction even though you're playing a real character. It's the same kind of approximation of somebody; it's just your interpretation of them.

'I don't really feel like I was playing Dalí when I was doing it, but I felt, as much as I could, the sense of him, what his ideals were, and what his fears were. I don't feel like I was doing an interpretation.'

'I had this whole series of photos,' he added, 'and figured out the way he would move his body. There's a picture of him pointing. I spent days trying to figure out, "How did he get his arm like that?" It was the first time that I ever really got into characterisation, trying to work on movements. I was doing tons of stuff on his walk and such. It was probably unnecessary, but it was the one time I felt, like, slightly satisfied. But I want to bring that intensity to every job.'

Talking about his lead actor's performance, Morrison said, 'He did a good job of capturing that noncommittal aspect of Dalí, who wasn't

committed to the Lorca relationship, nor was he fully withdrawn.'

The film explores the relationship between Dalí and the openly homosexual Lorca. Dalí has said that while Lorca was 'madly in love with me' he didn't reciprocate. However, the film's writer Philippa Goslett is convinced the pair had an intimate relationship. 'Having done a huge amount of research, it's clear something happened, no question. When you look at the letters, it's clear something more was going on there. It began as a friendship, became more intimate and moved to a physical level, but Dalí found it difficult and couldn't carry on. He said they tried to have sex but it hurt, so they couldn't consummate their relationship.'

Director Morrison is more cautious. 'First of all, it's not known if they were lovers. Dalí was always ambiguous about it. I don't think there's anything documented about Dalí having homosexual relations. He did have a great deal of curiosity about other people's sexuality. He liked being voyeuristic. These other things are not known, but one imagines from the elasticity in his own identity that he could have been bisexual.'

Of filming the gay love scenes, Morrison said, 'Sex scenes are always difficult to shoot, uncomfortable and technically difficult because you're dealing with something that is very personal and intimate, so you need that emotion but you also have to reduce it.'

'I thought I'd never get another acting job again,' Robert said. 'So I was like, "Yeah – why not try to do something weird?" There's all these gay scenes and, you know, I haven't even done a sex scene with a girl in my whole career.

'And here I am with Javier [Beltrán], who plays Lorca, doing an extremely hardcore sex scene, where I have a nervous breakdown afterwards. And because we're both straight, what we were doing seemed kind of ridiculous. Trying to do it doggie-style. Trying to have a nervous breakdown while doing it doggie-style. And it wasn't even a closed set. There were all these Spanish electricians giggling to themselves.'

Regardless of these temporary difficulties, *Little Ashes* gave Robert the perfect chance to act in artier fare. 'I didn't want to get stuck in pretty, public school roles or I knew I'd end up as some sort of caricature. Playing Dalí has been a complete turning point for me. It's the first part I've had that has required really serious thought. I became completely obsessed with Dalí during the filming. He was the most bizarre, complex man.'

Robert also found something he could identify with in what the movie's characters went through mentally.

'I guess what *Little Ashes* is about is the kind of fear of letting ambition go too far and being too concerned with public image and then forgetting who you are and not being able to actually feel or

experience anything new afterwards. I'm always very aware of that. If people are talking about you, people that you've never met, you eventually become very paranoid about things and you feel like you can't be honest with new people and you're always weary of them. So I guess I learned to avoid having too much of a mask and to try to be as honest as possible.

'If you get a few hits every now and then, you deal with that when it comes. I think you're much better off trying to be yourself as much as possible and holding on to some kind of semblance of yourself than being terrified of other people's judgment. I learned a lot of things but I guess that's one of the things that would relate to my situation.'

Predictably, most of the media attention was focused on Robert's love scenes rather than the film itself. Talking about this shadow, British actor Matthew McNulty, who plays director Luis Buñuel in the film, remarked, 'Possibly to people that haven't seen the film, but I'm not really bothered about that. If people want to judge it before they've actually seen it and judge it on the fact that there's a teen heartthrob playing the lead then more fool them. I think that the film has got merit of its own through its writing and the cinematography. Hopefully word of mouth will dispel any of that.'

Reviews for *Little Ashes* were mixed. The *Hollywood Reporter* wasn't smitten with the film,

although it did concede that it is 'often enjoyable to watch' and praised Robert's performance, saying he 'captures the initial shyness and growing flamboyance of Dalí'. Acclaimed US film critic Roger Ebert said the movie was 'absorbing but not compelling'. The *Guardian*, however, was less impressed, saying that Robert 'struggles to portray the hugely complex Dalí with any real conviction.'

Overall though, *Little Ashes* was a success for Robert – both professionally and personally. Career-wise it was certainly a leftfield choice and a bold one. But, more importantly, it was also a role that erased any remaining doubts that he had over his ability as an actor. He put so much into the part that he became the character. It made him realise that acting was definitely the job for him. He now had the ability to play different kinds of roles.

Ironically, just as he was beginning to think about carving a career out of playing leftfield characters, he was about to sink his teeth into his biggest and most mainstream role yet.

chapter seven

Robert Enters the Twilight Zone

'I thought Edward was impossible to play.' – Robert Pattinson

Following Robert's personal triumph with *Little Ashes*, his agent was determined to get him back into Hollywood's good books. 'She said, "Listen, you haven't been here all year – you've got to come and do some casting auditions,"' Robert recalled. 'So *Twilight* was just one of the casting auditions I did. I really didn't expect to get it. I didn't know how big it was either. Now it has ended up being this huge thing, so it was just a complete fluke, I guess.'

The film opens with the sombre voice of Bella, played by Kristen Stewart, as she intones: 'I've never given much thought on how I would die, but dying in the place of someone I love seems a good way to go.' As opening lines go, it's a pretty good one,

considering how much it reflects the mood of the surprise smash of 2008.

While it may feature creatures from another world, *Twilight* is essentially an old-fashioned love story of two star-crossed lovers – in this case high school girl Bella Swan and a vampire called Edward Cullen. Told from the perspective of Bella, *Twilight*'s incredibly heightened and angst-ridden look at high-school romance was lapped up by teenage girls, who swooned over the voyeuristic, first-person narrative and the sweeping, epic tale told by first-time author Stephenie Meyer.

While it was no surprise that Meyer's hugely successful novel was to be made into a film, the question was: who was the right person to do it justice? Summit Entertainment turned to director Catherine Hardwicke to adapt the book for the big screen. She had already impressed with the handling of the complexities of female teen life in a critically lauded indie film – 2003's *Thirteen*. She was to prove the right choice, as her keen eye caught Edward and Bella's smouldering looks and lustful glances perfectly.

Hardwicke was acutely aware of what drove the story. 'Edward loves Bella and wants to protect her – that's everybody's fantasy. And there's sexual tension. They can't go too far or he'll kill her, which is this tingling, exhilarating thing!

'It's temptation and desire... we're trying to

convey a great love story about this girl, a heightened passion, and that first love where you'll do anything. Who doesn't remember writing the person's name 8,000 times in their notebook and watching and figuring and planning every minute as to how you'd get a glimpse of that person at school, where even if they brush against you in the hall it's magic? All that stuff Stephenie conveys.'

As soon as Hardwicke got the job she knew straight away that there was going to be one part that was going to prove incredibly hard to cast. 'Edward was the big problem. How do you find the best-looking guy in the whole world that everyone is going to think is great-looking, but he has to be believable to be a 17-year-old in high school?

'That takes out almost every hot actor you can think of. They are not high-school boys. And then he has to be pale skinned, and that eliminates a whole other group. And it's weird, he has to look otherworldly – and so many cute guys came in, but they all looked like you could see them at your high school. Or "Hey, that looks like the guy on our football team" or "He looks like the prom king at our school" and that's not what you want. You want someone who you believe was not a normal person – who had that special quality and he had already lived 109 years and had this internal torture.

'So that's super-challenging. And we did the big search. And then it was becoming kind of scary to

not find anybody. So I'm on the phone, talking to Rob in London and this was just a way-out choice. I'd seen *Harry Potter and the Goblet of Fire*, but I hadn't met him. It was getting down to the wire and I was like "Who is this guy?" and it was kind of dodgy on the phone as we were trying to figure each other out.'

Asked if he had read the books before his meeting with Hardwicke, Robert admitted, 'Not in their entirety before getting the script, no. I did my screen test, had the weekend before my next meeting for it, and read all three over one weekend. I obviously really liked them, but it is always strange reading a book knowing that I am hopefully going to play the part. It's read in a very different context.'

Even before his official screen test, Robert recognised how great this character could be. Following the example of actors like Elijah Wood, who had filmed his own audition tape to land the part of Frodo in *The Lord of the Rings* trilogy, Robert decided to do the same.

Robert and a male friend re-enacted the chemistry class scene where Bella and Edward have their first proper conversation. Unsurprisingly, Robert's attempt at charming his male friend didn't quite compare with the chemistry he would end up having with Kristen! Once he'd seen the finished results, he was so embarrassed he refused to send it in.

Getting the part of Edward was going to be

hard. He had to see off thousands of hopefuls to land the role and worst of all, he still had no real idea how to play the character. At the time Rob thought that Edward was just window dressing, and he actually put off the audition for months because he thought that it was essentially going to be just a modelling job.

'I basically spent two months thinking, "OK, how can I play this character like he is written and be absolutely nothing like him in real life?"' he told *Vanity Fair* magazine. 'How can I get away from the most major aspect of his description – his appearance?

'As it is written from Bella's perspective, she describes him in this obsessively lustful way. She does not see a single flaw in him at all. It's a very traditional aspect of first or young love. So it took me ages to think of it, but it ended up being really simple: if you are in love with someone, you can't see any flaws in the other person. So I finally figured out that I didn't have to play the most beautiful man on the planet, but just play a man in love.'

It was a shrewd observation that ultimately won him the part – although Robert still didn't fancy his chances on the day of the audition. 'I was literally embarrassed walking into the audition. I thought that even going into the audition was completely pointless, because they were just going to cast a model or something. I felt it was kind of arrogant of

me to even go in. I was almost having a full-on panic attack before I went to the screen test,' he said.

'I thought Edward was impossible to play. You can only play him as a 2-D blob, some piece of man meat – a bland thing where people can project whatever they want on to you. I didn't know how to do that. I didn't even bother getting a six-pack. So even in the audition that was part of it, "Take your shirt off" – and I was like, "If that's the context, I'll tell you right now I won't get it."'

Playing a role based on looks was something that Robert had experienced when playing Cedric Diggory – who is described in the book as 'absurdly handsome' – so it's something he generally steers away from. 'It kind of puts you off a little bit when you're trying to act, and you are trying to get good angles to look good-looking and stuff. It's really stupid and you think, "I'm really egotistical." But I think that's the most daunting part about it.'

In fact, he was so nervous about auditioning for the part of Edward that he ended up taking the anxiety-combating drug Valium in a bid to ease his nerves. Talking to GQ, he said, 'It was the first time I've ever taken Valium. I tried to do it for another audition, and it just completely backfired – I was passing out.'

He needn't have worried, because his screen test impressed Hardwicke, who instantly felt a spark between Robert and Kristen. Robert thinks that it

was his instant chemistry with his co-star that won him the part.

'I know they were casting for ages and I was one of the last people they saw. I just went in and I had a connection with Kristen. I think it was because I so expected it to be different to how it turned out and expected the girl who played Bella to be so different to Kristen, that I was genuinely shocked when she did her performance.

'I thought it was going to be a real damsel-in-distress actress, and of course Kristen is tough, smart and a good actress. So it completely changed my opinion and I ended up playing him as a kind of a wreck. That was how that happened.'

Producer Greg Mooradian recalled of the casting process, 'On the fan websites, every single person who'd read the book had already cast the film for you 20 times over. We did take a look at their ideas and we decided we were never going to please everybody, so what we had to do was go with our guts. The actors we cast are the actors we feel best embodied these characters.

'It took forever to cast this movie, but once we found Bella and all of the Cullens, I realised we finally had it. When I actually got to see them together performing in a scene, it took my breath away.'

Talking about the audition scene, which famously saw Robert act with Kristen on Hardwicke's bed, Rob remembered, 'I was reading, going, "OK, there

are two lines in this" and then we make out and I try to kill her. It's like, "I've known you for an hour." It was funny. I think I must have gone way over the top with it as well, because I remember looking up afterwards and they were just looking at me, going, "What are you doing?" Catherine said I looked like I was having a seizure.'

Robert got the part, but incredibly, unbeknown to the film's bosses, he had actually been having second thoughts about whether he would say to yes if the role was offered to him. Luckily, Kristen's involvement in the film helped convince him.

'It was the first job that I wanted to do in ages. It was the environment of the audition. I thought that it couldn't have been something more than just another film. All these books which make even the slightest indentation on the market are immediately bought and made into films and I didn't want any involvement in that. But having Kristen there, because of the way she was in the audition and because of her track record – especially since she's so young and having made really good choices – got my interest.'

It shows how different Robert is from other young actors. While most actors would do anything for such a part, Robert was trying to decide whether the film was right for him and not vice versa.

Talking to *Life Story*, he said, 'I thought that it could have very easily ended up being very campy

and cheesy. Not that the book was. I thought that there was a lot of stuff in the book that could make a really good movie, but I was certain that I was going to go the audition and there would be a bunch of big muscle guys outside and there'd be a really silly little girl there. I just thought the whole thing was going to be really silly, but she really shocked me when I went in to audition.

'I didn't want to do a stupid teen movie. I specifically hadn't done anything which anyone would see since *Harry Potter*, because I wanted to teach myself how to act. I didn't want to be an idiot.

'This came kind of randomly and I didn't really know what it was when it first started. I was going to wait for another year. I wanted to do two or three more little things and then do something bigger, and then this happened and I was like, "Well, OK". I had done another movie which I'd gotten really intense about before and I felt kind of satisfied afterwards, much more satisfied than I had from other movies.

'I don't know what the result is from getting intense about something, but you definitely feel more satisfied. I wanted to take that into *Twilight* and also try to break down the assumption [that] if a movie is being made from a book that it's just to make money. I didn't want to be involved in something like that. But I thought Catherine and Kristen would be supportive of that. So I wanted to make it by the time people got to [the film's location in] Portland

that I knew everything about everything. I wanted everything to be right.'

He added to New Zealand teen magazine, *Crème*, 'When I first read it when it wasn't so hyped, I think one of the things, the initial appeal, [was that] I thought this is weird. It's like Stephenie Meyer's fantasy. It seemed like the author thought she was Bella – there are so many things about Edward's character that were so specific. So in a lot of ways you feel very voyeuristic and that was one of the strange things which put me off it, to be honest, but then when I started doing the job that's what I liked about it.'

One of the hardest obstacles for Robert was playing a character when the series' fans already had a clear image of how he should be. 'Even though there was the book *Twilight* and there seems to be an abundance of information, it makes things no easier. The only thing you can do if you're playing it is to try to find the right parts that you can relate to. It's not like I'm playing the book. So many people who have read the book probably think I'm doing it totally wrong compared to how it was written.

'The only thing that you can take from the book is the general outline, the mood changes, the emotional changes and development. I'm not playing it exactly as it is in the book. I think it's impossible.'

When Robert was announced to the world as playing Edward Cullen, Stephenie Meyer said, 'I am

ecstatic with Summit's choice for Edward. There are very few actors who can look both dangerous and beautiful at the same time, and even fewer who I can picture in my head as Edward. Robert Pattinson is gong to be amazing.'

Meyer admits that at first she had no idea who Robert was when the producers told her they were thinking of him as Edward. She recalled, 'They told me that they have got this guy and he's interesting. So I Googled him and I thought, "OK, this could work." Then I saw him in costume and he was the Edward I saw in my mind.'

The fact that Robert was British would have undoubtedly helped. While there would initially be a mini-uproar from fans when it was announced that it was to be a British actor playing the part of Edward Cullen, Meyer always believed the character should be played by someone from the UK.

Robert explained, 'The author's choice was an English guy, which was really strange. She wanted all-English guys to play Americans. I think there is something about this myth in America of British actors.'

One of the many actors who tried out for Edward Cullen was Dustin Mulligan, who stars in the remake of *Beverly Hills 90210*. 'Unfortunately, I didn't have a British accent, so, I didn't get the job,' he joked.

Indeed, Meyer's first choice was British actor

Henry Cavill. During the movie's early development, Meyer posted on her website, 'Indisputably the most difficult character to cast, Edward is also the one that I'm most passionately decided upon. The only actor I've ever seen who I think could come close to pulling off Edward Cullen is Henry Cavill. Henry was Albert, the young son in *The Count of Monte Cristo*. Can you see it? I know I can!'

But Cavill was already 25, and with a potential four-film franchise it was going to be increasingly hard to keep him looking like a 17-year-old boy. When it became obvious that Cavill was too old to play the part, Meyer wrote, 'The most disappointing thing for me is losing my perfect Edward. I'm not willing to relinquish Henry completely. ... I propose that Henry play Carlisle!' But she was to lose that battle as well, with Carlisle Cullen – the patriarch of the vegetarian vampire Cullen family – going on to be played by Peter Facinelli.

Asked later about his near-involvement with the *Twilight* franchise, Cavill said he was surprised to be so well thought of by Meyer. 'I've heard this, but I haven't heard from Stephenie. I haven't spoken to her personally, and I haven't spoken to the producers. What I've heard, or pieced together from various sources, is that Stephenie had seen me in whatever jobs I had done previously, and I was probably perfect then. But then, the ravages of time had taken their toll!'

But Meyer got over Cavill quickly enough and entrusted Robert with something very valuable indeed. To get more into character, Robert was given a sneak peak of what was then one of the most eagerly awaited publishing events in years – *Midnight Sun*, a novel that would retell the story of *Twilight* from Edward's point of view. It has now been abandoned until further notice after the first few chapters were leaked on the Internet. Robert jokingly insists it wasn't him!

'I am definitely the only person apart from her and the director who has read it,' he told MTV at the time. 'Just me and Catherine. It is very top secret. And it is like halfway, two-thirds finished. I read that right at the beginning [of filming], I got a lot of stuff out of that.

'It's exactly the same events, but a couple of other things happen. You get the same gist, but it's funny how different things affect Edward in ways that you don't really expect if you have just read *Twilight*.

'I based a lot of my angst from that on the character. It's talking about how little control he has. In the book it seems that when he says, "I'm a monster and I'm going to kill you" and she says, "I'm not afraid" you kind of know the whole time in the book that he's never going to do anything bad. But you read the first chapter of *Midnight Sun*, where the full extent of how much he wanted to kill her and how he's considering

killing the entire school just so that he can kill her, becomes evident.

'I wanted that element of him to be very prominent. I wanted Bella to be saying "I'm not scared – you won't do anything to me" but not with such certainty. So that it would suddenly be like, "You won't do anything to me…will you?" I wanted something like that. I think it makes it sexier if there's a very real chance of him just flipping out and killing her.'

What surprised Robert was that he had understood the character more than he realised. '[It turned out] we had the same perspective!'

He added, 'Edward obviously didn't want to be a vampire. He was turned to a vampire when he was unconscious, woke up in this purgatory state, which he doesn't appreciate.

'Someone that you don't know has put you in this situation which is very difficult to understand. When someone has given you eternal life when you've already accepted you are dead, and also you have to kill people, you're always going to have to live with that. Also you have infinite memory because you're a vampire, so you're always going to be wrapped with guilt. When it comes to the big fight between bad and good at the end, he essentially fights the good and bad in himself.'

'Things like his anger – he seems like a nice guy but in his head there is so much resentfulness and

anger. When you look at it from [Bella's] perspective he's like the perfect and nice guy, but in his head he's doing everything wrong: "Just by being with this girl I'm being a selfish bastard – I'm putting her life in danger every second. I'm pathetic because I can't stop being around her." I really liked that.'

Clearly, Edward Cullen was a character that Robert really enjoyed playing, and it came as something of a surprise considering he thought it would be just another hunk role. On examining the character more closely, he was delighted to see that it was as complex as any other part that he had played before.

'What I never really understood about his attractiveness, especially to young girls, is his gentlemanliness. I thought that teenage girls like the dangerous aspect of males, and so I tried to emphasise the danger and make the more gentlemanly side of this character a veil to something else underneath. I really tried to make him an incredibly strong and powerful character, but at the same time self-loathing and extremely vulnerable.

'When his life is put into basic terms, he has nothing to live for and all he wants to do is either become a human or die. The only reason that he hasn't died is because he is too scared; he doesn't think he has a soul. Then he meets Bella, who makes him feel like a human and feel alive again. At the same time, her human vulnerability makes him

incredibly vulnerable, because even with his super speed and his super strength, he still can't fully protect her. Whenever she is in danger, he is in danger. If she dies or goes anywhere, then he is gone, too.'

There is a moving flashback scene in the movie, which sees Peter Facinelli's character Carlisle turning Edward into a vampire. The scene is meant to show Carlisle's reluctance to place such a burden on the young Edward, but he has no other choice as he doesn't want Edward to die.

Facinelli thought it would be a good idea to whisper something into Robert's ear when he bites him – an intimate moment that only the two of them would hear. Facinelli revealed not only what he said but also how it would be something different each take. He started whispering, 'I'm sorry' then 'Be reborn, my son.' But after a few of these takes he started messing around by saying, 'Rob, you're so sexy.' Facinelli insists that the reaction shown in the movie is from that line!

Because Robert had had such a positive experience on *Little Ashes*, obsessing over every minute detail of the character, he was determined to do the same for Edward – to the point that it sparked disagreement between Robert and the character's creator.

'I was talking to Stephenie Meyer saying the guy must be chronically depressed,' revealed Robert. 'And she was saying, "No, he's not, he's not." But I

still maintained that he was. I mean, not like depressed, but just this sort of loneliness. When you see him at school, he doesn't really talk to anyone. He must get bored after a while only hanging out with the same four people in his life.'

Meyer gave her side of the story, too. 'With Rob, we sat before the filming started. It wasn't an argument but we did actually disagree on his character. I'd be like "No, this is how it is." He's like, "No, it's definitely this way." Yet in the performance he did what he wanted, and yet it was exactly what I wanted.'

'He's a very mesmerizing person to be around,' she added to *Entertainment Weekly*. 'He's got such a compelling personality. I don't think you'd want him for a boyfriend. And you couldn't just be his friend because he's terribly sexy!'

Despite the debate with Stephenie, Robert's intensity actually helped to lighten the mood on set, as the cast and crew bonded over their mischievous aim to try and get the serious actor to laugh. They would follow him around, reciting passages of the book, which showed the lighter elements of Edward – an aspect of the character that he tried to steer away from as much as possible.

'I tried to play [him] like a 17-year-old boy who had this purgatory inflicted on him. I just thought, "How would you play this part if it wasn't a teen book adaptation?"'

Kristen remembered, 'I had this little thing: "Rob,

let's just rehearse the scene all the way through without tearing it down and criticising it." We'd get two lines out, and then he would say, "No, no, no, it's not working." Rob made himself crazy the whole movie, and I just stopped and patted him on the back through his neuroses.'

Robert's total immersion in the character impressed *Twilight* producer Wyck Godfrey greatly, however. 'Rob Pattinson did so much personal work to create a character who has been emotionally dead for a few hundred years but is reawakened by Bella. He created a whole life for this character that went above and beyond the call of duty.

'You had to be sensitive around him, because it was kind of a dark and sad place to be. Catherine and everyone gave [him] space to do these very intimate scenes. There was the pain and addictive quality of him basically wanting to just reach over and kill Bella, an impulse he's fighting every moment he's with her. Rob played the character as being tortured, which is really the metaphor for young love – it hurts, it's great, it's maddening. He brought that element to it. He becomes obsessed with her, the same way she is with him.'

Even though Robert had been hired in part because of his dangerous, alluring looks, the studio bosses, believe it or not, still had some problems with his facial features. His eyebrows had to be trimmed and they made him fix his teeth.

'They wanted me to have the perfect smile,' Robert recalled. 'I never thought anything was wrong with my teeth. But the producers still wanted me to wear a brace. They were like, "Wear this thing the whole time when you're on set." I was like, "Oh, this is going to be a nightmare!" I didn't do it, though. I was lying to them for about two months saying I was wearing it. They were like, "Wow, that's incredible. You can't even see it!"

'The lenses were the most annoying thing. I don't wear contact lenses in reality. I couldn't figure out how to get them in through the whole shoot. It took me, like, 20 minutes to get them into my eyes every morning. It's 5.30 in the morning and you're poking your eyes for 20 minutes. It's so annoying. The happiest day of my life was throwing them away at the end. I couldn't wait to get them out.

'You know, I was so ignorant of everything in the beginning. I literally went in thinking this was just a drama, not a fantasy film, not a vampire film, and not even a love story. It's a serious drama. So when they started doing all these make-up tests for the vampire stuff, every single time I was shocked by it. Initially they wanted me to wear very long, Anne Rice vampire hair, down to my waist. I wasn't allowing that to happen.'

While the early publicity shots of Robert sporting short hair had pleased studio chiefs, director Hardwicke wanted to experiment with longer hair to

see what it would look like. Hair stylist Mary Anne Valdes said, 'If Catherine really liked the long hair, she would talk the studio into it. The hair extensions went on that day and we took them out the next. We agreed [it should be short]. But Catherine had to see for herself that the short hair was best. If she hadn't seen the long hair, she'd still be wondering.'

Robert was delighted that they didn't keep him in long hair. It wasn't the first time that he'd had problems with the wardrobe department. During a costume-fitting for *Harry Potter and the Goblet of Fire*, he recalled, 'I hadn't done anything for six months so I was a little unfit. I remember the costume designer saying, when I was trying on swimming trunks, "Aren't you supposed to be fit? You could be playing a sissy poet or something." The next day I got a call from the assistant director about a personal training programme!

'The stunt team are the most absurdly fit guys in the world. I can't even do ten press-ups. I did about three weeks of that, and in the end I think he got so bored of trying to force me to do it that he wrote it all down so that I could do it at home.'

Unfortunately, Robert ended up incurring a shoulder injury and had to stop his training regime. His low levels of fitness figured again on the set of *Twilight*. 'I got injured on the first shot of the first day. I wasn't even doing a stunt. I was just trying to pick up Kristen, and I almost tore my hamstring

because I hadn't been doing enough squats. It was very embarrassing.'

One of the famous scenes in the film is the dramatic aerial courtship of Edward and Bella. Recalling scenes in *E.T.* and the *Superman* movie of the 1970s, we follow their relationship soaring through the air (figuratively and literally) as Edward shows Bella the height of his powers. The audience shares Bella's gasps as he leads them on a dizzying trail, jumping from tree to tree through the forest until they reach the top of one tree, dangling precariously.

While that scene was filmed with real people and not done with special effects, they not surprisingly used stunt people rather than Robert and Kristen. And a good thing in hindsight, as director Hardwicke revealed. 'The scene with the pair on a the tree were stunt doubles. They had to climb up there by themselves. There was a lucky escape because when the helicopter came to film them, they were nearly blown off as it swooped past them!'

Not that the pair didn't get their hands dirty. In another thrilling sequence, the scene in the school's parking lot, we see Edward spring into action when an out-of-control van speeds towards Bella. With his superhuman speed, Edward gets to her in time and shields her with his strength. It was a particularly dangerous scene to film, but special effects chief Andy Weder had some tricks up his sleeve.

'The van was on casters, twelve-inch diameter

wheels, and on air bags that held the whole thing up about an inch above the ground. We basically built a steel frame and cut the bottom of the car out and mounted the wheels. To do that, we had four guys pushing it like it was sliding,' he remarked in the *Twilight* Movie Companion book.

And to achieve the crushed-door special effect?

'We formed the aluminium over the real door to get the shape to match it perfectly. Then we flame-cut a big hole out of the middle where we wanted the dent to be, and put these sheets on top of that so he could bend and push that section back. All the cables and such like were digitally erased later.'

The climax sees a violent and animalistic fight scene between Edward and evil vampire James (Cam Gigandet) in the dance studio that Bella used to go to as a child. Despite it being the film's final action scene, it was one of the first to be shot.

Stunt co-coordinator Andy Cheng noted, 'For the fight, we had to figure out what it would look like. Catherine and I ended up calling it "animal style". The idea was the good vampire, Edward, is not violent; he doesn't want to fight, until James [attacks Bella]. That turns him crazy. We watched videotapes of tigers – how they lunge and attack, how a panther runs – we did the research, then [artists] storyboarded the fight, and [we] shot a rehearsal to show Catherine and the producers.'

The scene where Edward bites the vampire's neck was not done with special effects. 'When Robert is biting me they wanted it to look meaty,' Gigandet recalled. 'So they used chicken and honey on our bodies. Then we ran out of chicken, so they stuck Swiss cheese on my neck. Trust me – after a day under the lights, neither of us needed garlic to stay away from each other.'

At the end of the shoot it became clear to Robert how close they had all become. When filming had finished – at the scene when Edward drives Bella back to her dad following their date at a restaurant – Robert went back to his trailer to chill out. Putting on a DVD, he suddenly burst into tears. It was then that he knew how important this film had become to him.

It wouldn't be the last time that he would burst into tears regarding *Twilight*. As the promotional hype started to gain momentum on the film, he found himself being noticed more and more. There would be large crowds screaming at him, but he didn't quite react the way most people would.

He explained to *Moviehole.net*, 'I don't know why it still shocks me. I mean, I've been going for the last three weeks, just going to different cities all around the world, just to get to these planned mobbings, where everybody just screams and screams and screams. But every single time, I get so nervous, kind of cold sweats and everything. Every single time.

'I started crying in Italy. Like, completely involuntarily. You know when you have the wrong reaction to something? It was really embarrassing. I didn't even know I was doing it. Kristen, I think, turned around to me and she's like, "Are you crying?" So, yeah. I started crying when people are screaming at me. I really didn't think that would happen.'

Speaking at the film's London premiere, a completely stunned Robert said, 'I just turn up to places and people scream. That seems to be my job. It's like, "Here I am. 'Arrghggh!!'" That's all I do.' As he was saying it, he was drowned out by even more screaming. 'See?' he told journalists.

While Robert had been given a taster of the rabid affection following the build up to the film and its subsequent release, he was to find from this point on that the fans were going to get louder and the spotlight on him was going to get brighter. How would such a private person as Robert cope with such attention?

Pat Yourself on the Back

'I am a quiet, private person. It's strange. You have to change a little bit.' –
Robert Pattinson

If Robert was unsure about how much things were going to change, he very much knew after a trip to a DVD rental store. 'I was in a Blockbuster on the day *Twilight* was being released. I had forgotten it was being released that day. There were two families who had come with eight- or nine-year old daughters to get their *Twilight* DVD. They were standing in the line crying and I stood watching what all this commotion was about. They didn't know I was there or anything. I was just thinking, "Wow, you're crying about a DVD." It's fascinating.'

His Aunt Diana echoed these sentiments, saying, 'Rob's gobsmacked by all the attention he's getting. He's very cool about it all, but he can't believe it either.'

Not that Robert was a stranger to attention from fans. In the days following *Harry Potter and the Goblet of Fire*, he said, 'Somebody asked me for my autograph the other day. Because I finished school and I'm not really doing anything at the moment, I was just kind of aimlessly wandering around London, and these two guys who were about 30 came up and asked for my autograph. I was really quite proud at the time, and they wanted to take photos and stuff.

'I've been to a couple of Warner Bros premieres in the last few weeks and considering no one knows who I am, it's still a pretty scary event. So I don't know what it's gonna be like when you actually have to do something rather than just walk in. I still trip over my feet and stuff when I'm not supposed to do be doing anything. So, I'll just see how it goes. I'm looking forward to it.'

Looking at the reticent Robert now compared to the eager young actor then, it seems like they're two different people. But Robert does admit that he was seduced by the fame side – for a short while at least. 'I've changed so much. I'm not nearly as cocky as I was. I was a real prat for the first month. I didn't talk to anyone.'

His *Little Ashes* co-star McNulty remembered that Robert was bashful when he would get recognised for his work in the *Harry Potter* movies. 'There were times when we'd have girls come on set

just to get an autograph and he was as baffled as anyone. He was like, "Oh, right, OK." I think, had it been after *Twilight*, it would have been a completely different story.'

Robert has now become a pop-culture phenomenon, a star whose reach extends around the world. Cooper Lawrence, author of *The Cult of Celebrity*, explains that the attraction of Robert to his female fans extends beyond the obvious reason of his good looks. 'He's edgy but not too edgy. He's someone you can still bring home to Mom, but he's a little down and dirty so you think he's cool. And he's so non-threatening, and that's a big part of it.'

A couple of obsessive fan incidents left a burning impression on Robert. 'A mother recently gave me her baby and asked me, "Can you please bite her head?"!' he told *OK!* magazine.

Another one saw him being accosted by four women who 'had scratches and scabs into the side of their necks, so it was freshly bleeding when they came up to get a signature. They were like, "We did this for you." I didn't know what to say. I was like, "Gross!"'

Robert also revealed the lengths that fans have gone to get a glimpse of their idol. 'People ambush me and try to figure out what hotel I'm staying at, as well as wanting to touch my hair. Everyone just screams and screams. It still feels surreal.

'I've been getting recognised from this since the

day I finished shooting *Twilight*. It's crazy. The weirdest thing is that even if I'm wearing a hat and sunglasses people still come up. [To me] it's like "What are you recognising?" Maybe I just wear the same clothes all the time. I don't normally go shopping and things like that, and those are the places it happens. I've been uncomfortable in crowds my whole life. I've always felt that everyone is looking at me.

'So this doesn't make any difference. I could be in a supermarket and have a full-on panic attack when there's no one else there.'

When out celebrating his 23rd birthday at Vancouver's Global Grill and Satay Bar with his family and co-stars, he was stunned to find the place besieged outside by fans who had learned of his whereabouts. 'Because of Internet stuff and Twitter, there will be a crowd if you are in a place for more than half an hour,' he told the *Daily Record*. 'I've learned never to stay in the same place for more than 20 minutes.'

All this attention comes a shock for Robert, as he has always downplayed his looks with a dry, caustic, self-deprecating remark. 'I never really considered myself attractive. I was always kind of gangly in school. Before I go out to face a crowd, I stare and stare at myself in the mirror until I have to tell myself to stop staring, since there's nothing I can do.'

Apart from Robert, Kristen and now Taylor

Lautner (who plays Jacob), the rest of the cast have been able to dip in and out of the worldwide buzz whenever they like. They can sample the crazy, heady atmosphere without having to live the day-to-day attention that the main stars receive.

Facinelli said, 'I didn't get as much recognition from the first movie, which is kind of nice. I could walk down the street and get a cup of coffee, but Rob couldn't go anywhere. He had to go into hiding.'

That's not to say that they're strangers to a bizarre autograph scenario every once in a while. 'I was in Hawaii floating on the deck, lying in the sun, and I had my two-year-old daughter napping on my shoulder. Some girl swam out there and asked, "Are you Dr Carlisle?" It was really funny.'

Robert is nevertheless grateful to the *Twilight* fanbase, calling them more devoted than even *Harry Potter* fans. 'There is this strange kind of connection that some people have to the books – it can be pretty extreme. I think there are fans of *Harry Potter*… that are like that as well, but I guess this story is just so intimate that people think they really know the characters and can feel the emotion.'

Because of his *Harry Potter* history, Rob has managed to take tips from a young cast on how to stay grounded. 'I don't have too many concerns because it's just so new to me now. My only concern is when something is so hyped up and you're really being put on the front of things, people instinctively

want to tear you down. That's scary when you're not really putting yourself out there. You're not saying, "Hey, look at me!" but people put you on stuff and when you don't know if you're ready for that or not, that's what's scary about it.

'I think the way the kids from *Harry Potter* are dealing with fame is by ignoring everything and just living their normal lives as much as they can. That has really worked for them. They're all very sane. I think Daniel lives in the same house he grew up in, in London. You can just see he has matured. He just wants to do good work. There's nothing else to it. You don't have to be in LA. Well, sometimes you do but you don't have to go to clubs and stuff.'

However, Robert still can't quite get to grips with the level of mass hysteria that seems to follow him around. 'The biggest challenge is coping with the crowds. I am a quiet, private person. It's strange. You have to change a little bit. Walking down the street comes with screaming.'

Mass fan attention has led to some hairy moments, too. The making of the drama *Remember Me*, the first film Robert worked on since the *Twilight* franchise began, has become more synonymous with such mobbing than its content. Several media outlets printed pictures of Robert having to evade a mass of screaming young females just so he can go from the film set to his trailer, which is sometimes only a few feet away.

One occasion saw Robert witness the riskier side of having so many fans. He was walking to his trailer in New York with his security team when a large crowd of screaming girls started running towards Rob. What started off like a scene from the Beatles movie *A Hard Day's Night*, where the band flee from girls though the streets, took a more scary turn when Robert ended up on the road, where he was struck by a taxi.

News agency Reuters reported, 'Pattinson was clipped on the hip in front of a bookstore in Manhattan where he was shooting scenes for his new film, *Remember Me*, a drama about two young lovers dealing with family tragedies. Flanked by five security guards, the British actor tried to run past a group of teenage girls when the accident happened.'

Luckily Robert was not seriously hurt and was back on set in no time. But it's not known who was more emotional – a shaken Robert who had had a lucky escape or the girls. 'You see what you did? You almost killed him!' yelled one of the bodyguards.

The incident led New York Police officials to criticise Robert's security team. 'Enough is enough. His security people aren't up to the task of keeping him safe, and they have no idea how to deal with the crowds this guy attracts,' a police source told *irishcentral.com*.

It's not just everyday folk who have a crush on Robert either. His allure stretches to the celeb world. Talking about her crush on him, Paris Hilton said, 'I

just saw *Twilight* last night for the first time, and I have to say that I think Rob is a beautiful man and an amazing actor. He's fabulous! I just didn't get it before, but now it all makes sense. I really enjoyed the movie and loved watching Rob in it.'

Megan Fox, who was once voted sexiest woman on the planet, said, 'I just wanna be pretty like he's pretty. I want that James Dean, that sexy-ass hair.' Teen star Miley Cyrus, who had earlier said she didn't see what the fuss was about, posted on her Twitter site, 'Gave a hug to Rob Pattinson today. OK girls, I get it now. So cute.'

Even male celebrities were quick to sing Robert's praises, although not about his looks. '[Mickey Rourke] once came up and said that he really liked the trailer [of *New Moon*]', Robert said. 'That was the weirdest thing and the most surreal experience I've ever had. The only two celebrities who've come up to me to comment on it were him and Zac Efron, who are at opposite ends of the spectrum.'

And it's not going to end. *New Moon*'s producer Wyck Godfrey said that things got so crazy filming in Italy that they struggled to keep Robert from 'getting torn limb from limb'.

Thirsting for his Blood

'I was in a restaurant during a break, and when I came out two hours later, 500 people were waiting for me at the exit.' – Robert Pattinson

Hard to believe now but there was a time when *Twilight* fans didn't agree with casting Robert as Edward Cullen. When the decision was announced, a large group of the series' fans went straight to the blogs to vent their anger, with some calling him 'ugly'. Stephenie Meyer admits that the initial fan backlash to Robert 'broke my heart'.

Speaking before the *Twilight* movie was released, she said, 'Because I've had my tiny bit of celebrity, I'm aware of how hurtful those things can be. I apologised to him for ruining his life. He said his mom was sending him links like, "Oh no, they called you a gargoyle!" They just raked him over the coals. The way he took it was a lot more positive than the way I would've handled it. He was like,

"I'm going to prove them wrong. I'm going to go out there and prove them wrong."

'The movie hasn't come out yet and he's won over 99.9 percent of the people who didn't approve of him as Edward. And when they see the movie, oh my gosh, there's no way not to love him! It's really too bad in some ways because *Twilight* is going to be limited by the fact that this is a vampire romance and it's basically aimed at teens. If not for that, his performance in my opinion is Oscar-worthy.'

Strangely, Robert seemed to agree with the fans' doubts about his casting. 'There was a huge, universal backlash about my being cast as Edward Cullen. Seventy-five thousand *Twilight* fans signed a petition against me.

'I completely expected it. That's the reason I didn't want to go in for the part initially, because it's really putting yourself out there. You say, "Oh, yeah. I think I can play this part – the perfect guy, best-looking guy in the whole world." It was like, even going in for the audition, I felt like a bit of an idiot. I felt pre-judged by anyone who turned up to the casting. I mean, I just thought even having the gall to go in means you're a bit of an arrogant p***k.

'I was quite happy when the reactions from the fans were a hundred per cent negative. I was like, "Thank you. I'm not perfect." All the blogs were like, "He's a bum." I was like, "Cool. I guess I'm going to be a character actor."'

Director Catherine Harwicke had no such doubts though. 'We needed someone who was both pretty and scary,' she said. 'The one guy that kids were all saying they wanted for Edward was Tom Welling from *Smallville*. He's beautiful but could you ever imagine being afraid of him? We did not have a good option until Rob came along. And the movie rests entirely on his shoulders.'

Even the studio was unsure at first, Hardwicke recalled. 'There was a call from the head of the studio asking: "Are you sure you can make this guy handsome?"' she told *GQ*.

Just to prove how fickle some people can be, it was only months later that R-Pattz mania began. But as much as he was being heralded as the next big thing as *Twilight* approached its release date, it wouldn't have meant anything unless the box office reflected the hype.

That it did without a doubt. In the USA, *Twilight* knocked James Bond's *Quantum of Solace* off the top spot at the box office, and made more than $70 million in its first three days – a staggering figure for a modestly budgeted movie. It was also the most successful opening for an independent film yet.

Hardwicke knew Robert was a star in the making, even encouraging the fans to be more vocal. 'I think it's awesome. Most of the time in our lives we're supposed to behave properly, fit in a box and do what everyone tells us to do and you go to a

premiere or a football game you get to scream. You get to have fun. That's so cool!

'To me, Rob is really like an otherworldly creature. I think it'd be awesome if he created a whole strange and interesting character, like a Johnny Depp with weird Tim Burton characters. He's also a beautiful musician. He's a writer, pianist, and guitarist. I think he's kind of great. I've been amazed when I've been in the studio and watched him sing and create music,' she added.

Even so, Meyer feared for Rob's sanity, knowing that his whole world was going to change following his decision to play Edward. 'There is going to be a group of girls now who will follow his actions from now on. I asked the producer, "Is Rob ready for this? Have you guys prepped him? Is he ready to be the It guy?" I don't think he really is. I don't think he sees himself that way. And I think the transition is going to be a little rocky.'

She couldn't have been more shrewd in her judgement.

'I feel for Robert,' his co-star Peter Facinelli added. 'He didn't sign up for this knowing what it would become; the fan base has grown ever since we filmed it. There were underground fans when we started. I remember we'd all go to their website and they said, "All these actors are wrong for the roles. Facinelli doesn't have blond hair, what are they thinking?" For Rob he just signed up thinking it'd

be a cool little movie. All of a sudden he's like the James Dean of today.

'That's a lot to put on a guy's shoulders, but hopefully he'll be OK. He's kind of nerve-racked. He doesn't like to leave his apartment a lot. But I think it'll be good. This will bring good things to him.'

Following the film's release, there was huge surge in interest in Robert, reflected in him topping many, many best-looking male polls. One found Robert being named Sexiest Man In The World by *Glamour* magazine in August 2009. More than 2,000 people voted in the poll, which saw Robert beat the likes of Brad Pitt, George Clooney, Hugh Jackman, Johnny Depp and *High School Musical*'s Zac Efron.

The magazine's writer Karen Krizanovich stated, 'Robert Pattinson's tall lanky frame is sex appeal in overdrive. He's got cheekbones, dangerous eyes and a mane I'd run barefoot through – but it's his modesty and charm that knock me sideways. One look and I have to cool off before I do something rash – like board a plane and track him down.'

Not that Robert is unduly affected by it all. 'The hottest actor stuff doesn't really mean anything,' he said. 'You have a month maybe with all this heat and hype and, if you don't capitalise on it, someone else will.'

He certainly capitalised on it when he was asked to introduce a segment with *Mamma Mia!* star Amanda Seyfried at the 2009 Academy Awards. It

was a night that Robert aptly described as surreal: 'What train did I get on to get here? It was so ridiculous, and it just got even more and more ridiculous. I go there and then I'm sitting in the second row. It was unbelievable. I kept thinking that something terrible is going to happen. I was thinking that the whole time. I just used up all my luck, so I'm probably going to die at 23 or something.'

His co-star Kristen Stewart was rumoured to be co-hosting with him but she apparently pulled out, with her dad saying, somewhat icily, that his daughter would present at the Oscars 'when it's a great movie, not just one that makes a lot of money'.

It got even more ridiculous a few months later when Robert attended the 62nd annual Cannes Film Festival. There was Beatles-like hysteria as crowds went crazy for him. Some of the world's biggest names might have been in town but it seemed the media and audiences only had eyes for Robert.

Two lucky fans at the festival got a souvenir that will linger long in their memory. Attending the charity amfAR's Cinema Against AIDS charity event, Robert was to help the cause by contributing something at the celeb auction.

'The 23-year-old actor was sitting at a table when movie mogul Harvey Weinstein suggested Robert sell a smooch. He was shocked by the impromptu auction, but agreed to take part to raise money for charity,' reported TheBosh.com. Robert's kind-

hearted gesture not only gave two teenage girls a story that would make them the envy of their friends but he also raised $70,000.

Weinstein, who has organised the gala for years, said, 'Rob Pattinson – I made him kiss girls in Cannes! He's the most charming, wonderful young man. He really cared about the charity, and that's not an easy thing to do. That's a sweet, sweetheart thing to do. And then we got two bids.'

Talking about his Cannes experience to France's *Premiere* magazine, Robert said, 'I was in a restaurant during a break, and when I came out two hours later, 500 people were waiting for me at the exit. It was total chaos. But I'm sure that if I'd said to one of those girls, "Come on, let's go have breakfast," she would have been totally embarrassed and would never scream my name again.'

Robert's whole life had changed but it was not quite clear if it that was a good or bad thing. On one hand, he had gone on record saying he is a private person who wants to make arty films rather than mainstream blockbusters, but on the other he plays along with the star image, makes sure he signs autographs for his fans and spends time Googling himself to see what people think.

'The Internet feeds the worst part of your soul. When you have nothing to do, when you're too tired to read a book, you go on. I'll read the news, go on to the *New York Times*, and [then] get bored and go

on IMDB. Then you realise how pathetic you are. I have to delete my history [of websites visited]. It's kind of addictive, but at the same time pathetic.'

Speaking during the early *Twilight* hysteria, he said, 'I'd like to think I haven't changed much. Within myself, I don't think I've changed. When I go out on the street I look down more often. It's been extraordinary. I don't think anyone expected this, especially as it seems to keep building and building. Comic Con [the 2008 film and comic convention] was the eye-opener and it's just got bigger and bigger, which is an interesting thing to deal with.

'I think it's still really young with me so I don't see any [negative] aspects. I still live the same life but I just get recognised. It's not the worst thing in the world.'

Robert even got the one thing that any star dreads – a stalker. But we're not sure many deal with a supposed stalker the way Robert did. 'I had a stalker while filming a movie in Spain last year,' He told *Crème* magazine. 'She stood outside of my apartment every day for weeks – all day, every day. I was so bored and lonely that I went out and had dinner with her. I just complained about everything in my life and she never came back. People get bored of me in two minutes.'

Despite such protestations, no one was getting bored of him. It seemed everyone wanted to know about *Twilight*, and Robert Pattinson in particular.

Not surprisingly, the constant attention soon began to take its toll on Robert.

For someone who is a self-confessed loner, the realisation that he won't be able to have the same freedom that he once loved and took for granted must be a worrying one. 'I can't remember what my normal life is like,' he admitted during the promotion trail for *New Moon*.

Struggling with the paparazzi attention, Robert sighed, 'I was quite a paranoid person anyway, so it doesn't really feed well when people are looking at you. I'm not really in the right job. I don't like having my photo taken. I don't like the attention. I think someone follows me. They do the most random stuff. I get a photo taken through a burger drive window, and it's like "What?" They always seem like they're six feet away. I don't understand. I'm walking around and I don't see anybody.'

In an interview with France's *Premiere* magazine, he talked about having to hire security guards. 'I feel like a weasel when things like that happen, like the world had to revolve around me. I have to look over my shoulder all the time, be super-vigilant, because at any moment, someone could be filming or recording what I'm saying.

'It makes me feel like working non-stop: at least on sets, the level of security gives me a bit of privacy. It's a relief. I haven't even found one place in the world yet where I could disappear. Even the most remote

places I can imagine someone will ask me for a picture with them or an autograph.'

Normal life looks to be further and further away, because at the moment Rob is the hottest actor on the planet and that means lots of press attention and lots of fans. This is something that worried director Hardwicke. She even admitted to feeling guilty about her part in transforming Robert and Kristen Stewart from rising actors to superstars.

'I mean, part of me feels kind of guilty because they are both such indie spirits... so independent,' she explained. 'I feel bad for all the craziness. I don't think [they enjoy this limelight]. They are really artists, they like making meaningful art, interesting art. So I hope they can find a way to do that, let the frenzy die down.'

Michael Welch, who plays Mike Newton in the films, added, 'Rob Pattinson and Barack Obama are the two most famous people in the world. I don't see how this is sustainable – is this gonna keep going for the rest of his life?

'Is it time to start getting concerned here? It's tough, man. I don't know where his life is really headed. I don't wish I had Rob's life at all. I'm glad he's OK. And as long as people don't start ripping into him and breaking him in two, I think he'll be OK. I wish him the best, and hope he's going to be all right.'

Love At First Bite

'I always like a kind of madness in a woman, and when they are really, really strong.' – Robert Pattinson

R ob may be coy about his looks but as his mother has stated, he has always been popular with the ladies. So it should come as no surprise that as he was propelled into the A-List, the speculation over who was really dating Robert intensified.

There was *Push* actress Camilla Belle. The two are friends, but that still didn't stop the rumours of there being something more. In fact there was a twist to the tale, with Rob being branded a home-wrecker for ending Belle's relationship with singing star Joe Jonas – a tag that was levelled at Belle when it was rumoured that Jonas broke up with singer Taylor Swift for her.

Rob was quick to defend her honour, however. 'I'm friends with her. Camilla's the nicest. She's a

saint. And it's funny that she's being portrayed as this home-wrecker. She's literally the most unlikely person to be a home-wrecker. It's just ridiculous.'

'We have a big group of friends,' Belle explained. '[Robert] is very cool – a very nice guy.'

Rob not only gets linked to friends, but also to people that he doesn't even know, such as *Transformers* beauty Megan Fox. 'He's outrageously attractive – he's a very pretty man,' was her response. 'I've never been in a room with him, though, so those rumours aren't true. Although, you know, every other girl on the planet wishes that it was, but I didn't have the opportunity so…'

Other girls that Rob is rumoured to be dating include LA resident Erika Dutra, who he met at the amfAR charity event in Cannes, and American TV actress Shannon Woodward. He was even rumoured to be flirting with *Star Wars* star Natalie Portman at the *Vanity Fair* magazine Oscar party.

Speaking about the kind of girls he likes, Rob said, 'The stuff I find attractive in women, I always regret finding attractive. I always like a kind of madness in a woman, and when they are really, really strong. And they're the worst mental strong women.'

If we mention Robert and his dating habits then we have to mention a certain co-star. Because not only were Robert and Kristen Stewart involved in one of the biggest on-screen romances of recent times but rumours also quickly began to circulate that they

were as close off-screen as they were in front of the cameras. The talk delighted some fans of the series, while of course disappointing others.

It's no surprise that Rob and Kristen should be so close considering how the two essentially lead *Twilight*; their closeness was evident even before cameras began rolling. 'We sat around my dining-room table for, like, two entire nights with the script,' revealed Kristen – to which, Robert replied, 'Two nights? It was more than two nights!'

'Well, it was actually all preproduction,' admitted Kristen. 'But there were two nights that we were actually, like, productive.'

One of Robert's gambits to break the ice was to jokingly propose to her on several occasions. 'I mean, I don't know how serious he was, but yes,' joked Kristen. 'We spent a lot of time together, a lot of, like, really heightened time.'

'It used to be my thing,' Robert explained. 'I would propose all the time. Just go up to someone, you know, and say "I love you" or ask them to marry you. It always works.'

It is no surprise that everyone wanted them to get together – the chemistry between the pair is palpable. And Hardwicke, who made the pair do their audition on her bed, says it was there from the start. The audition scene was the one where Edward finally tells Bella who he really is. The way Robert played it was with an incredible amount of stillness

to ensure that all focus was put on the words, without any unnecessary movement to distract from the power of the atmosphere.

Not everyone did it that way. '[One] threw a pillow at my head,' Kristen said of the other hopefuls. 'People were trying to get the anger out of the scene, being very aggressive. Not Rob though, he played it very simple. That was what was cool. Everybody did this really theatrical thing like using the whole room but [he] just stood there and said [his] lines.'

'Kristen did three scenes with them [the other actors],' Harwicke recalled, 'and we did the famous scene on my bed. When Rob and Kristen did that scene and I'm filming it, I just knew. There was no question that these two had the chemistry, the intensity and could match each other. It came alive. And my attitude was "OK, done, this is our guy."'

Kristen agreed, telling the director right there and then after he left that it 'has to be Rob'.

Talking about the occasion, Robert said, 'Casting was really easy-going, and Kristen is also very cool, but at the same time there is something very, very serious about her. I really wasn't expecting the girl who plays Bella to be like her at all. Her professionalism made me keep my mouth shut whenever I wasn't acting. It further gave the illusion of being serious.'

Kristen was actually one of the main reasons that

Rob went to the audition. 'I read the scripts and I barely even knew that they were books too. The only reason I went to the audition was to see Kristen, because I'd just seen *Into the Wild*.

'Kristen being in it was like – it was my insurance. I mean, she was on a good roll of classy jobs. And so when I found out she was doing it, I was like, "Well, this isn't gonna be a silly movie. Because why would she want to do a silly movie when she was on a roll?"'

Kristen recalled, 'Everyone came in playing Edward as this perfect happy-go-lucky guy, but I got hardcore pain from Rob. It was purely just a connection.

'Rob came into the audition looking sort of terrified. The pain was just very evident in him. I am not saying it's in Rob, but he knew what to bring to that character. We didn't need the statuesque model types who come in and just pose. I couldn't see any of the other guys [playing the part]. They weren't even looking at me. It was like they were focusing on their lines, but Rob is very organic. He's in the moment and he let it happen, which is brave. He's a courageous actor.'

She added to *GQ*, 'Everybody came in doing something empty and shallow and thoughtless. I know that's a f**king great thing to say about all the other actors – but Rob understood that it wasn't a frivolous role.'

However, Kristen promised fans of Robert that kissing him was not all it was cracked up to be. 'He has the thickest beard. You didn't notice until five minutes afterwards, and then you're like, "Oh, wow. I think I'm bleeding. I think I'm totally raw,"' she told *People* magazine.

In a sign that showed how much news Robert generates, even his body hygiene was being discussed in great detail. *GQ*, who interviewed him for a cover shoot, described his clothes as smelling like 'he has recently purchased them off the back of someone less fortunate than he.'

One *New Moon* source told E Online, 'He stinks. I mean, it's awful. He never showers, and it drives people on the set crazy. He completely reeks.'

Not that Robert cares, shrugging, 'I don't have much of a sense of personal hygiene or styling or anything.'

Odour aside, it was no surprise that they have been linked to dating in real life. Just witness the screams of delight from fans when the pair went up to accept their best kiss prize at the May 2009 MTV Movie awards. At one point they gazed longingly at each other before they closed in together and – as the audience held their breath – quickly recoiled, turning to the microphone and cheekily saying, 'Thank you.'

Both have been at pains to deny the dating rumours. Robert insisted he is 'young, free and single' while Kristen added, 'It's just totally false.

Robert and I are good friends. We went through a lot together, so we feel very close. But if we go out in public, every little detail is scrutinised, like the way I stand next to him. I know the guy really well. It's only natural that we sort of lean on each other, because we are put in the most psychotic situations.'

Of course, at the time when the rumours started she was still in a relationship with Michael Angarano, who she met on the 2004 TV movie *Speak*, when she was 13 and he was 16. However, it wasn't until three years later that they began dating. 'He was older than me. I never thought I'd date an actor, but he's my best friend,' she has said.

On another occasion she added, 'He's older than me – he's 20 now – but when you're 13 and he's turning 16, it was always sort of an out-of-reach thing. Then you get a little older and you realise, "Oh, what the f**k am I thinking? I can have you like lickity..."' she laughed while snapping her fingers. 'He's awesome.'

Asked whether Angarano, who shot to fame playing Jack's son on TV show *Will and Grace*, was bothered about her on-screen kisses with Robert, she insisted, 'He's been an actor much longer than me, and he's done all those things. So it's fine.'

In fact, Angarano could have also been a *Twilight* star alongside Kristen: he was offered the role of Mike in the first film. 'Michael was going to be in the

awkward position of being jealous of Edward. It was a little close to home,' explained Hardwicke.

Kristen has since split up with Angarano, which not surprisingly fuelled the rumours about her and Robert. The pair didn't help the situation with things like Robert saying that his celebrity crush is Kristen and she telling MTV, 'I mean, he's outrageously attractive, he's like a very pretty man.' Another interview saw her quoted as saying, 'Oh, he's like a little tortured artist. He's British, he's tall, he always looks like he's thinking about something and he's quite witty. So he's pretty sexy.'

Sources continue to insist that Rob has had a crush on Kristen ever since he met her. 'He's a total ladies' man,' a source told the media. 'She's unattainable, and that makes her attractive to him.'

Even Hardwicke added fuel to the fire. 'I cast them together, so obviously I think they're awesome together. There's no question about that. [...] They are both amazing with very interesting minds.'

She added to celeb blog *Allie is Wired*, 'From the first moment they met, you could feel the magnetic pull and sexual tension. That's essential to transfer to the big screen.

'I do feel lucky directing Kristen and Rob, because their faces are so beautiful. They're expressive, their skin is just porcelain, and sometimes I am literally watching the monitor and I'm going, "Oh I'm so excited." Just jumping up and down. But I don't

want to say anything, because I want to keep them in the moment. Sometimes I feel like getting gold here. And it is very exciting.'

Co-star Ashley Greene (who plays Alice Cullen) said of the pair, 'The chemistry is incredible,' and *Twilight* screenwriter Melissa Rosenberg described it as genuine. 'When I wrote *Twilight* I didn't know who was starring in it, so I wrote in a vacuum. There was some rewriting that had to be done when we knew who they were, because I had started with more of a comedic edge and it wasn't appropriate for those actors and the tone.'

Not everyone was so happy with the idea of them being a couple in real life. Following news that Kristen had split with her boyfriend, Robert's aunt Monica Nutley expressed her disappointment about rumours of the pair getting together. 'I don't think it would be a good idea for Robert to be in a serious relationship with Kristen,' she said. 'How can he live his life with a fellow star, with their every move being watched just like Tom Cruise and Katie Holmes?

'He's only 23 and probably won't get married until he's 40, if he's got any sense. I think he will eventually come back home to England and fall in love with somebody he's known since school.'

It might come as a surprise now, but despite their instant chemistry, Robert almost jeopardised the relationship – by trying too hard to impress. 'In the beginning, I thought to myself, "Because she's so

serious, I've got to be really serious." I didn't speak to her for about two months so I would seem really intense. I would only ever talk about the movie. And I kept recommending all these books. It didn't really work though. Then I started falling apart and my character started breaking down. I felt like an idiot just following her around, saying, "You really should read some [French writer Émile] Zola, and there's this amazing [French director François] Truffaut movie."

'And she started calling me on things: "Have you actually watched this movie?" "Yeah." "What's it about?" "It's about a guy on a train." "Did you just look at the photo on the cover of the DVD?"'

Nevertheless, countless articles, blogs and video news stories have been dedicated to the possible romance between Robert and Kristen – or Robsten, as they have been nicknamed in the press. Whether they were spotted together at a bar in Vancouver or glimpsed cuddling at a Kings of Leon concert, they were rumoured to be getting cozy together.

But it also seems no female cast member in *Twilight* is safe when Robert is around; having also been linked with his co-star Nikki Reed (who plays Rosalie Hale). Even more bizarrely, website *backseatcuddler.com* claimed that the pair went on a double date with Kristen's then boyfriend. Sometimes it's hard to keep up.

It gets even more convoluted with the appearance

of Emilie de Ravin. It's been heavily reported that Robert has been getting cozy with his *Remember Me* co-star, who is most famous for her role as Claire in the TV action drama *Lost*, much to the apparent jealously of Kristen.

Robert meanwhile laughs off all the rumours. 'The movie is so insulated. Someone was saying it's like being in the eye of the storm. When you're in it, you can't really feel anything that's going on. It seems like complete calmness. Then you look at magazine covers, and you realise it's actually a real magazine cover with rumours that we're together. It sounds stupid, but people seem to believe it.'

Getting annoyed with all the speculation, Kristen's on-screen dad Billy Burke, said, 'If they want to date each other, fine. Look, when you're that age, you're going to make mistakes. You're going to date people you probably shouldn't date. It's all part of the growing process.'

He also told *E! News*, 'As far as I know, I'm gonna say bull. I'm not buying it. Please!'

Of course, with any great screen romance, audiences want to believe that the passion they saw on screen is reflected off it. This means that they are watching something of substance rather than simply great acting. *Twilight* fans are desperate to see Edward and Bella in love for real.

That need to see Kristen and Rob together isn't going to go away any time soon. Celeb magazines

pack the newsagents' shelves with huge, blown-up images of Robert and Kristen accompanied by headline grabbing words like 'Pregnant' – 'Engaged' – 'It's Official: They're Together' etc. – with no real evidence to back up their claims.

But if the magazines sell, then they'll keep printing stories about their supposed romance. And you can't imagine *Twilight* fans being tired of reading about them together, so we'll no doubt be hearing about them for a long time yet.

Another String To Robert's Bow

'Music is definitely my back-up plan if acting fails. I don't want put all my eggs in one basket.' – Robert Pattinson

It turns out that Robert is also a hugely talented musician, playing guitar and piano, as well as being equipped with a fine and distinctive singing voice. 'I've been playing the piano for my entire life, since I was three or four. And the guitar – I used to play classical guitar from when I was about five to 12 years of age. Then I didn't play guitar for like, years. About four or five years ago, I got out the guitar again and just started playing the blues and stuff. I'm not very good at the guitar, but I'm all right.'

Another musical genre that Rob tried his hand at was hip hop. 'When I was 14, I fronted a rap trio. [It] was pretty hard core for three private school kids from suburban London.' Unfortunately his rap

career came to an end because their hardcore street image took a battering when Rob's mum came popping into the bedroom to see if they wanted some more sandwiches!

'I've really gotten into hip-hop again recently,' he says now. 'I'm reliving my childhood. I've been listening to a lot of Wu-Tang Clan. I always wanted to be a rapper when I was younger. That's always what I wanted to before I started acting.'

Robert's home town of Barnes not only has an acting legacy thanks to its theatre companies but it has also put its stamp on music history as well. It is home to Barnes studios, which have welcomed the likes of Madonna, Coldplay, Beatles and the Rolling Stones. The nearby Bulls Head pub is described as the 'suburban Ronnie Scott's' thanks to internationally renowned jazz players plying their trade there. On a sadder note, Barnes also has a footnote in musical history for being where T-Rex frontman Marc Bolan died in a car accident.

Apart from rapping, Robert is also in a group called Bad Girls. Talking about the band he said, 'Bad Girls belonged to my first girlfriend's current boyfriend. He was having an open mic night and he invited me to sing, but it was just a bit of fun.

'We only played a couple of gigs. It's just a couple of friends of mine and some other people that I had met fairly recently. We just wanted to start a band for something to do. A lot of my friends are actors

and have so little to do all the time, so instead of just being bored, we were like, why not start a band? So we did. I had kind of roll-on, roll-off musicians. I still try and play, but it's weird now.

'I grew up with some amazing musicians in London who are still my friends,' added Robert. 'Marcus Fosters, Bobby Long and Sam Bradley are recording their albums now, but Johnny Flynn (a folk singer) completed his one a while ago. I just saw him play in LA and he was incredible. But he's always been incredible so I can't say I was surprised. The album is great; no one else does music like him at all.

'Music is a big part of my life, not enormous. I go through phases, especially when I'm in London, where all I do is play music.'

If Robert's acting career hadn't taken off, he was convinced there was only one job he would do. 'I wanted to play piano in restaurant in the South of France. I went on holiday there once and I saw this guy in his tuxedo and he was playing. He had a glass of whisky on top of the piano and was sitting there looking so depressed and I was like, "That's the coolest thing I've ever seen." And I played in some pizza restaurants for a few years, and it was the coolest thing I've ever done.

'I still find it very, very therapeutic. It's the most relaxing thing you could possibly do.'

If you're lucky, you might spot Robert at a

karaoke bar. 'I used to love playing live at open mic nights and at bars,' he revealed. 'I could go completely nuts and be completely free. It's a cathartic experience for me.'

Just make sure you don't record it, however. 'I did a couple of gigs and people filmed them and put them on the Internet. It just ruins the whole experience. You're like, "Oh, that wasn't the point." So I stopped. I'm going to wait for all this to die down before I start doing live gigs again.'

Classically trained Robert briefly considered a career in music but has decided acting is the main focus in his life. 'Music is my back-up plan if acting fails. I don't want to put all my eggs in one basket,' he told the *Los Angeles Times*.

Ironically, it is his acting talents that have managed to showcase his music ones. Two of Robert's songs, 'Never Think' and 'Let Me Sign', featured in *Twilight*, although Robert was somewhat reluctant to have them included for fear of a backlash from fans thinking it was a cynical exercise.

'That's what I was scared about. It looks like I'm trying to get a music career out of *Twilight* or something. I've never really recorded anything – I just played in pubs and stuff – and I really didn't want it to look like I was trying to cash in. I hope it doesn't come across as that. I'm not going to be doing any music videos or anything.'

The decision to include the songs in the film was

Hardwicke's, after she kept hearing about how musically talented he was. 'I heard a little on Nikki (Reed's) computer,' she revealed. 'Then I said, "Oh Rob, why don't you come home to my friend's house and record a few tracks? Who knows where it could lead?"

'So we went over to my friend's in flip-flops and shorts to a house on Venice Beach. The guys laid down, I guess, six tracks and we took them and played them against scenes in the film, and there were two scenes I just loved, where Rob just, you know, killed me in the film.

'So the restaurant scene when Bella and Edward have a date, in the background you hear one of Rob's songs, it's called 'Never Think'. It's a really personal love song.'

Hardwicke added, 'I cried the first time I heard the two songs. They're deep, they're very soulful.'

'I didn't write it for the movie,' said Rob of 'Never Think'. 'A friend of mine wrote lyrics to one of the songs years ago, and I wrote another one with another guy a year ago. They were just recorded on my computer and I think Nikki Reed gave it to Catherine. She put it in the cut and asked me to look at it. And I thought it looked kind of cool. I didn't really think about it. I didn't even know that it was on the soundtrack until recently.'

'Never Think' was co-written by Robert and his childhood pal Sam Bradley. They had been friends

since they were kids at Tower House School, and it was singer-songwriter Bradley who had taught Robert how to play the guitar. They had lost touch over the years following Bradley's decision to move to Vancouver in Canada, but with Robert heading o to film *Twiligh*t in Portland – also on the West Coast, but in the US – it seemed like an ideal chance for the pair to reignite their friendship.

During their time together catching up and remembering past moments as kids, the two began to work on a new song – the tune that would end up being 'Never Think'.

'It started out as the best piano piece I've ever read,' said Robert. 'I came up with the song. My best friend wrote the lyrics for it and I made it into a song, and on 'Let Me Sign', me and another guy wrote. It was nice, and also helped my friends as well.'

'I'd never heard of *Twilight* and neither had he,' Bradley said. 'He told me as soon as he got it. He was just concentrating on making it as well as he could. What he said mostly was that he was going to be closer to Vancouver.

'Rob, when he plays music, he's really in touch with what's he's doing, so he plays a song differently every time. Any song, it never sounds the same. It's really cool, he's really in the moment. So the recording for 'Never Think' that he did will never sound the same again, which is kind of interesting.'

The second song, 'Let Me Sign' was used in an unusual place – the scene where Bella is close to death. Normally a big orchestral song would accompany a scene like that, but Hardwicke believed that Robert's voice would make it even more emotional.

'Everybody was really shocked when I said I wanted to put the song 'Let Me Sign' in Bella's "death" scene, in the ballet studio where she's dying with the venom and the blood. You don't expect it, but then you hear this song of deep anguish and pain and it's so powerful and beautiful.'

For the sensitive actor, the thought that someone was really interested in his music was a novel one. 'I sometimes played gigs by myself but generally I play in these tiny venues with no one watching. I never knew where they were going to put it; Catherine said she had put it in an unusual spot. I thought it was going to be in the end credits – you can put anything on the end credits but that's fine. But the mood of the song fits the mood of the scene.'

It wasn't just Catherine who was impressed with Robert's musical ability. The film's music editor, Adam Smally, gushed, 'Rob Pattinson is probably one of the most talented musicians I think I've ever met. He innately latched on the theme that Carter [Burwell, the film's composer] has written and it's just this beautiful little lullaby that bonds these two characters. It's kind of magical.'

One of the more famous scenes in *Twilight* showed

Edward serenading Bella with his piano skills. When they came to film that day, they had no music to give to Robert as the film's composer hadn't signed on for the movie at that point. 'So Rob made an amazing two-hour concert for us, just making some of the most beautiful music you ever heard that came just out of his heart,' said Hardwicke.

However, after impressing everyone, Robert was then asked to do it again weeks later – but this time playing Carter's theme. Understandably, it was something that didn't best please Robert. 'I think he wanted to kill us that day,' joked Hardwicke. 'But he's such a good pianist. I wanted the audience to see that it was him.'

The theme – 'Bella's Lullaby' – ended up becoming so popular that it's now been published as sheet music. Although it was written by Burwell, who said it 'represented adolescent sexuality', the composer was quick to praise Robert, calling him a 'talented pianist'. Praise indeed, considering Burwell's credentials. The composer is a regular collaborator on the Coen Brothers' films including *Fargo* and *Burn After Reading*.

Ironically, despite Robert's protestations that he wasn't ready to be a music star, the *Twilight* soundtrack, which features 'Never Think', went on to sell 165,000 copies – an impressive figure for a soundtrack album, and it ended up becoming Atlantic Records best-selling film soundtrack ever.

It's not difficult to believe that Robert's presence helped the sales. Robert said: 'I didn't really think of it beforehand. I didn't know it was going to be on the soundtrack or anything. I wanted to do it under another name because I thought it would be distracting, which it has been. So it's probably all been a big mistake, but I like the idea of it and I just think the song fits and I did not think it sounded like me. So I thought it would just work, but I don't know.'

Robert isn't the only one in his family with musical talent. His sister Elizabeth (or Lizzy) is a writer and singer, and has had three Top 20 hits – two with the dance band Aurora ('Dreaming' and 'The Day It Rained Forever') and one with producers Milk and Sugar ('Let The Sun Shine'). The last of these ended up at number one in the Billboard Hot Dance Club chart.

In fact, when Robert was messing about with amateur productions years ago, Lizzy was the acting star in the family. She appeared in several plays and even tried her hand at comedy, acting out sketches. But fate had other plans for her and she moved into the music world. Like her younger brother she started off singing in pubs and clubs around London, but while Rob went down the acting route, Lizzy was discovered by an EMI talent scout and within a year she was a member of Aurora.

Lizzy also features in *Twilight,* providing the

backing vocals for composer Carter Burwell's track 'Who Are They?' When Edward makes his dramatic introduction in the school canteen it's his sister Lizzy's 'cool, ethereal, mysterious voice' (according to Hardwicke) that is playing in the background. Although Kristen jokingly called it 'kind of creepy', she concedes that for Lizzy to sing for her brother 'is kinda right for the Cullen vibe.'

However, it's because of his sister's experiences that Robert has never been in a rush to enter the music industry. 'I don't think people should look for a contract. My sister works so hard to make money and I think it ruins you. I think it's a lot easier to make money in the acting world, not that it's easier but there aren't so many pressures on you. You don't have to be so humble, where in the music industry you have to really bow down to a lot of people to get noticed.'

It must have been a musical film set, because it was not only Robert who had talent. Jackson Rathbone, who stars as Jasper Hale, is in a band, while Nikki Reed 'plays a little guitar'. Kristen is also a guitar player, and is starring as singer Joan Jett in the biopic movie *The Runaways*. Rathbone's band 100 Monkeys played a gig in Vancouver during filming of *New Moon* and the cast, crew and author Meyer turned up to support him. They were impressed. 'Jackson Rathbone can really play guitar!' wowed Meyer.

When they weren't playing music, they would spend time going to watch it being made. 'Rob and I went to see Kings of Leon and they were really good,' remembers Reed. 'He's gotten me interested in that whole world. Van Morrison too. I went and saw The Raconteurs with him as well. Oh, and Aretha Franklin. I like a lot of old bluesy singers.'

'Rob Pattinson and Kristen and Nikki would do a lot of jam sessions,' Rathbone revealed, 'and Kellan Lutz [Emmett Cullen] and Ashley Green and Peter Facinelli would all hang out in the hotel room and play music and hang out on the set.'

Fans of the film can only hope that one day they will group together and form The *Twilight* Band!

Hardwicke was thankful that her cast were fans of music, because Robert and Kristen in particular would regularly help with choosing which songs they should use in the film. 'It's like a big, crazy family,' she said. 'Over the course of six months and 250 people, the family dynamics can swing from highly functional to depressingly dysfunctional. With some family members, you can't wait to say goodbye; others you miss dearly.

'I lived for those creative jam sessions. Our stars Rob and Kristen both had great ideas about music. Rob has recorded several songs for the film and Kristen suggested the final prom song, by Iron and Wine.'

It's not the first film in which Robert's singing

voice has made its way onto the soundtrack. *How to Be* saw him play Art, a struggling singer-songwriter who believes – mistakenly – he has a chance of making it big. 'The lyrics of his songs are so literal,' Robert explained. 'Art talks about having problems with his parents, and the lyrics will be like, "I'm having problems with my parents/I don't know what to do." It's very earnest.

'Art's trying to be a musician, but he's not good at all. He has the energy and the drive to try and be good, but he's just not talented. He plays songs with his guitar at open mics and things like that and he's awful. The soundtrack does kind of "dream sequences" of the songs which are very intricately arranged and show what he could be doing, but he never really reaches it.

'People are very honest when they're playing in front of an audience. Even when they know they're bad, they really feel the need to play in front of people. It's quite fun to play that in a movie.'

However, Robert admitted the part did pose some difficulties for him. 'It's funny: it's quite difficult to fake playing the guitar really badly when you know how to play it. That was one of the most difficult parts of playing the role. I've been to some open mikes in my life, and seen how bad some people are.'

Oliver Irving, the film's director, remembered, 'He downplayed how good he was. A lot of the time he

would turn out to have a really good technique and we told him he needed to play it more simply.'

In another interview, Robert reiterated that he wasn't planning on a music career. 'I wouldn't pursue it just now. It just seems a bit tacky, like I'm cashing in. If it was my movie and I had written it I wouldn't have a problem, but I don't want to do it on the back of someone else's work.'

But music will always be close to Robert's heart, and he hasn't ruled out trying it at some point. 'I definitely want to stick with acting a bit now because it's nice to go from not really caring about you to where it's turned around. It's nice to be on a level playing field with your contemporaries to get good parts, and it only happens sometimes. It would be a bit silly to throw that away now. In my mind at least, I've got like five years of solid work mode in my brain, and I don't really feel like taking a vacation.

'I'd really like to do an album one day, but there's such a stigma at attached to actors who release music. I may try and do it anonymously, or wait until I'm unemployable.'

However, there is one dream project that would see Robert's two abilities brought together: a movie biopic of his favourite singer. 'I'd love to play Van Morrison... but I doubt I would get the part. "Brown Eyed Girl" and "Wild Night" was my inspiration for doing music in the first place. I saw him at the Hollywood Bowl not too long ago. I'd

seen him five times before and he really pulled it out of the bag. He played like it was 30 years ago. He's still got it. He played the entirety of his album *Astral Weeks*. The whole thing was unbelievable. He was just as free as he was then. He was younger, which was amazing. I would love to do something with him now.'

But if he can't do that, could we possibly be seeing Rob as an *X-Factor* judge? The answer is yes if Dannii Minogue has her way. 'I've heard that *Twilight* star Robert Pattinson is a huge fan of *The X-Factor*,' she said. 'I know he now spends most of his time in America but my *X-Factor* crew would love to meet him – so he has officially been invited by the gang to one of the live shows!'

Watch this space!

chapter twelve
A New Moon

'She's trying to get over me, but it becomes an addiction.' – Robert Pattinson

Despite the success of *Twilight*, Robert was still unsure whether or not he would end up playing his character again. On *Twilight*'s DVD commentary, he joked, '[They've] made money now. [They're probably asking] Where's Efron? You don't need to cast £350 actors from London now!'

While it shouldn't come as a surprise to see Robert Pattinson return as Edward Cullen, nor should it be a shock to know that he still had insecurities about doing the character justice. 'For one thing I'm surprised how relaxed I am about the whole thing. I was really nervous, especially because of the expectations and everything, and the first one did so well. I was really freaking out. Last time I had zero expectations, but this time I'm kind of freaking out a little bit.

'I was really beating myself up about stuff on the last one, but because of its success, I feel I kind of know that I did a couple of things OK. I have some kind of foundation, which I know will at least please an audience... maybe.'

No such problems for Kristen Stewart, however. 'It was very oddly easy to get back into it, and I don't know why. Typically I leave a project and I have a grieving process. I can't let it go, and then once I do, I have to put it away because it sort of haunts you. But I think knowing that I had to come back, I just never let it leave me. Plus, she's a very distinct character and very straightforward. And I have the ultimate resource: I have a series of books that is so explicit.'

The sequel to *Twilight* was quickly green-lit. One reason was to capitalise on its success and satisfy the fans' demands. The other reason was more practical. For a series that features young-looking vampires who don't age, it would look a bit silly if the films were two or three years apart and the young actors looked noticeably older as a result.

'We're going to go as fast as humanly possible, especially since there are at least four stories to tell,' producer Greg Mooradian explained while putting the finishing touches to *Twilight*. 'We'd like to keep a real consistency as to how quickly we are able to do it. Some of the other stories are even bigger productions, so they require more prep time.

'It's been discussed. I can't tell you we're at that

place yet, but it's definitely been discussed,' he added, referring to the possibility of shooting back-to-back sequels, as with *The Lord of the Rings*.

Author Stephenie Meyer agreed, saying, 'I think that would probably be a smart way to do it. It makes sense in a world where actors are actually aging, and our characters aren't. That makes a lot of sense to me, but of course, we are still negotiating the contract on that.'

The main problem for the follow-up was how to get more screen time for Robert's Edward Cullen. That wasn't because Robert was becoming a diva, but more because the character is absent for a large portion of the book.

'When you look at the book, you wonder, "How is this going to work?"' pondered director Catherine Hardwicke, shortly before Chris Weitz replaced her. 'That's one of the balancing acts that is being considered. It's definitely an issue, because we all love that chemistry between Rob and Kristen, but that's also what's great about *New Moon* – he has to break himself away from [Bella], and the depression she gets into, the deep depression. That is the whole story, and you have to keep the integrity.'

The angle she was keen on was to abandon telling the story from Bella's eyes. 'That could be one of the ways,' she told MTV. 'Though his story was a little bit depressing; it seems like he just sat down in a room and (sulked). But, you can always make that interesting.'

In truth, the absence of Robert was a nightmare for the film's bosses. It had taken them ages to find their screen hunk after a long casting process, and he was hardly in the second book!

Intriguingly, the decision to leave Cullen out of many pages of *New Moon* was something that even Meyer hated, but it was purely down to her belief to always do what the character would do. 'As I started plotting *New Moon* it became clear that Edward was Edward, and he would to behave as only Edward would,' she explained in *Film Fantasy* magazine.

'I didn't want Edward to leave. I pitched a fit every bit as violent and tearful those I've seen in *New Moon* forums. Someday when *Midnight Sun* is available, I think you'll understand better what was going on in that boy's head.'

Melissa Rosenberg, the film's screenwriter, added, 'It's interesting. He isn't physically in *New Moon* a lot, but he is very much a presence throughout the book in Bella's mind, so Stephenie keeps him very much alive throughout the book. That was the challenge of the script, how to keep him alive in the same way the book does and stay true to the book. I think we found a way to do that.'

Kristen delighted the fans by saying, 'You will get more Robert Pattinson than you would expect.'

New Moon director Weitz agreed with Kristen's comments, saying, 'She spends a lot of the movie pursuing dangerous things to do so that she can

summon up this sense of him. So you see him quite a bit. And she sees him in the first act as himself until he decides – and this is a spoiler! – that it's best that they should be apart. Then she goes and rescues him in the third act. And the second act is a lot about her feelings about him and her memories and her dreams about him.'

'It's a separate voice in the book,' Robert added. 'Which would be kind of cheesy, so we've done some semi-apparitions, hallucinations,' he added at 2009's Comic Con event.

'There is one dream sequence that I don't think anyone will expect,' he told *Entertainment Tonight*. 'Edward is like this kind of demon. People are probably going to be like "What?! No, you can't do that!" So hopefully, people will get a little bit freaked out by that. I really want it to be disturbing.'

His presence in the movie was the thing he was most concerned about, he told *Film Fantasy* magazine. 'I really wanted it to be a complete absence, and everyone else is talking about my absence all the time. It's easier to give it more power at the end if I was completely absent. Now that it's added, it's very difficult to know how to play as little as possible without it being dead, but still keeping the kind of interest in it. I don't know if I'm expressing myself right. It's very difficult to play a figment of somebody else's imagination and I didn't want to saturate the film with my presence.

'There are a couple of dream sequences which I think no one will expect. They're just dark, bizarre. Bella has terrible nightmare. If anyone's had a nightmare where you wake up and you're in floods of tears after... well, there is a reason why she's crying. So we're trying to think of the most disturbing, almost nightmarish and horrifying ways to play it. Because I'm not playing Edward in those things, I'm playing a personification of her deep, deep insecurities, which I think she has a lot of in the book. So yes, it's quite fun to do that.'

Robert welcomed the fact that his character breaks up with Bella, as it represented a chance to do something different in the series. 'The scene where we temporarily break up – on one hand, it's completely impossible. And on the other, it sets a very different tone to the series. I think it will be good,' he told MTV.

It also turned out that Robert had always had a soft spot for the second instalment of the series, despite him almost being a supporting character in it. '*New Moon* was my favourite book. Mainly because Edward is seen in a romantic light, but in *New Moon*, the way I read it anyway, he's so humbled. He loves something too much but can't be around her so he deliberately tries and breaks it up, which I think is a very relatable and painful thing.

'The final scene sees Bella saving Edward. I just find it funny how everyone looks at Edward as the

hero but he's continually being saved by the damsel in distress.'

However, the main talking point was how the cast – who were incredibly close to Catherine Hardwicke – would feel about the new director, Chris Weitz. Hardwicke was to be replaced because of scheduling difficulties. Weitz was no stranger to fantasy epics following his work on *The Golden Compass*, but there were concerns that the tight-knitted cast might find it hard to warm to him.

'Everyone's different,' Kristen said about the change. 'Everyone asks me if it's different because he's a man opposed to a woman. That's like comparing apples and oranges. You can't define people like that. Everyone's different and you can't make generalisations. Chris is a very compassionate guy. If it's going to be a man directing the movie, he's sort of a perfect one because he is unlimitedly sweet and sensitive, and then, at the same time, willing to go there in terms of how dark the story gets.

Robert had no problems. Even before filming had started, he was publicly excited about the sequel. 'I think there's going to be some continuity, but it's weird, because they are shooting it in a different city than the first film. I've talked to Chris a bit, but we've only talked about my character; I haven't really talked about the whole look of it. But Chris is great with visual stuff, so it should be pretty impressive.'

'Aesthetically, it looks very different,' he added in

another interview. 'The script was very different. It's a completely different mood. So, I'm really interested to see how it works out.

'Catherine has such a specific style and such a specific atmosphere. It's a completely different mood in this one. Chris is great. I really like Chris. It's such a different film. Catherine has a kind of a purity about her and a kind of completely un-cynical viewpoint about the world. I think Chris is a little bit cynical and sort of looks at things in a little bit of a darker way. I think this a darker movie.'

Weitz was just as complimentary about his young actor. '[He's] a very thoughtful, clever, sort of diffident guy who was dealing very well, I think, with this extraordinary notoriety that has been thrust upon him.

'I think he is aware of the absurdity of the situation and he's not taking advantage of it, in a good way. I'm actually really impressed with both Kristen and Robert to the degree to which they commit to being faithful to the books and to finding reasons for the characters to behave the way they do in the movie. They're taking it seriously and they're not treating it like some kind of franchise or some kind of gag or some kind of gig that they're doing so that they get to do something else. They really want to make the best version of this possible.'

Joining the returning cast members were an abundance of new ones. Dakota Fanning and

acclaimed actor Michael Sheen in particular excited Robert when he was about to begin work on the film. 'I was really happy about the casting of those two,' he said. 'I think it's great. I think Michael Sheen is amazing. I think it's really, really good casting for it.'

But it wouldn't be the *Twilight* saga if there wasn't some drama. Robert got into trouble after cutting his famous locks before shooting began on the sequel. 'But what can I say?' quipped his co-star Ashley Green to E! 'I like guys with longer hair. I think he's getting enough flack, I'm sure. I mean, his every move is recorded and photographed and documented, so I'm not going to give him a hard time.'

Robert also managed to sustain an injury in the first scene he filmed, and had to have a thorough massage on his buttocks after pulling ligaments in his gluteus maximus. You can bet the lady who performed that job will dine out on that story for a long time!

And after finishing work on *New Moon*, Robert was just as wowed about his experiences with Weitz as he was on their first meeting. 'It wasn't just the director that made this one so different. We kind of know this animal that we're dealing with more. I have more of a supporting role in this one. I started three weeks after shooting and I did a lot of my scenes in an apparition scene where it was like one line of dialogue a week. So it was the most relaxing

job I've done. Chris has a very peaceful presence and I got on really well with him. I had a stress-free job. All the pressure was on Taylor!'

Indeed it was left to Taylor Lautner, reprising his role as Bella's friend Jacob, to fill in the hunk-sized gap left by Robert's absence.

New Moon begins the series' famous love triangle. Through Edward's absence, Bella seeks solace in the arms of Jacob – himself suffering from a supernatural condition. In Jacob's case, he's a shapeshifter – a werewolf.

'She's trying to get over me,' Robert said, 'but it becomes an addiction. The more I don't come back, the more she thinks "Should I settle for the compromise?" It's so depressing for Jacob, because you find the love of your life and you always know you're going to be second best.'

Not that he has too much sympathy for Jacob's character, preferring to highlight Edward's plight. 'I always thought that Edward feels like he's pretty much lost everything as soon as James, Laurent and Victoria enter the story. He didn't think about it before, but he's already on a downward spiral from that point and he's struggling to keep himself afloat, trying to deny things and trying to pretend that everything's OK. And so in this one, that's how he can leave so quickly. I always felt that he was expecting that he would have to leave in a short period of time.

Robert Pattinson was named UK *Glamour* Magazine's Sexiest Man Alive in August 2009.

Robert shot to fame by landing the role of Hogwarts-heartthrob Cedric Diggory in *Harry Potter and the Goblet of Fire*.

Above: With other Potter newcomers Stanislav Ianevski (Viktor Krum), Clemence Poesy (Fleur Delacour) and Katie Leung (Cho Chang).

Below: Robert with more of the cast.

It was as the vampire Edward Cullen in the hit movie *Twilight* that Robert found himself launched into superstardom.

Above: With co-star Kristen Stewart as his eternal love, Bella Swan.

Below left: Robert as Edward Cullen.

Below right: Edward and Bella at the Forks Prom.

Above: Nowhere in the world is safe for Robert now. He is mobbed by fans at the *Twilight* premiere in Germany…

Below left: …and again on the streets of New York…

Below right: …and once more in Japan!

Robert has had the opportunity to take on many varied and exciting roles.

Above left: Playing struggling musician, Art, in *How to Be*.

Above right: Robert as Salvador Dalí in *Little Ashes*.

Below: With *Remember Me* co-star Emilie de Ravin.

Above: Robert and Kristen reprise their roles as Edward Cullen and Bella Swan in *The Twilight Saga: New Moon*.

Below left: *Twilight* dominated at the MTV Movie Awards, winning awards including Male Breakthrough Performance for Robert and Best Female Performance for Kristen.

Below right: Stephenie Meyer, author of the best-selling vampire romance series *Twilight*.

Above: Kristen, Taylor and Robert at Comic-Con 2009 in San Deigo.

Below: The cast of *Twilight* on stage at the MTV Movie Awards.

Are you Team Edward?

Are you Team Jacob?

Above: Taylor got his first starring role as Sharkboy in *The Adventures of Sharkboy and Lavagirl*.

Below: He also appeared in *Cheaper by the Dozen 2*. Here he is at the premiere with Carmen Electra and Eugene Levy.

Taking time out to show off his martial art skills at the LA premiere of *The Adventures of Sharkboy and Lavagirl* in 2005.

Above left: Taylor plays Bella's best friend Jacob Black in the *Twilight* movie.

Above right: Blowing a kiss to fans at the MuchMusic Video Awards in Toronto, Canada.

Below left: With his co-star Kristen Stewart.

Below right: The two *Twilight* hotties together at the MTV Movie Awards.

Above: A still from *The Twilight Saga: New Moon*. Taylor's character Jacob Black gets closer to Bella.

Below: On set of *New Moon* with director Chris Weitz (*far left*), Ashley Greene and Kristen Stewart.

Above: Fans screaming for a piece of Taylor at the MuchMusic Video Awards.

Below: The *Twilight* cast at Comic-Con.

Above: Taylor on the set of his new movie *Valentine's Day*.

Below left: With another young and famous 'Taylor', Taylor Swift, his co-star in *Valentine's Day*.

Below right: Taking some time out of his hectic schedule to watch some ice hockey and cheer on the Detroit Red Wings at the Stanley Cup Final.

With his undeniable talent and dedication to his craft, the gorgeous Taylor Lautner is destined for great things.

'The whole concept I thought of was somebody who thinks everything is doomed, and he realises he's made another mistake and has to fix it.

'I don't think he's really mean. I think he's mean in the next one. I think in this one he's so... lost. He doesn't know what to do. It's this typically male attitude when you find somebody you're in love with and you just continuously, through your own doubts, keep messing up again and again and again.

'And then you realise as soon as you've messed up, you only have a few chances. But that's the good thing about Bella. It's not even giving another chance. She knows way more than he does about their relationship, and he just keeps sort of beating himself up about everything.'

It seems it's a character trait that Robert shares with Edward. 'I'm like that every time. I'll do that with every relationship I'll ever have. As soon as I like them I start beating myself up to the point of ridiculousness, and they hate me to the point of dumping me.'

The break-up scene in particular was one that Kristen found incredibly difficult. 'Before the scene, I was sitting in my car, like, f**king crying – crying so hard you can't breathe, because I was really overwhelmed and intimidated by the scene. Everyone says, "She better be able to pull off the emotion in this movie!" And it's such an important moment in the book, when he leaves.

'I'm thinking, "We have to be done now. Just tell me we're done."'

There is no doubt that the second movie featured some intense scenes, but the cast and crew insisted that it was a relaxed and happy set.

'*New Moon* was one of the happiest sets I have ever been on,' screenwriter Rosenberg enthused. 'The [driver] who picked me up said, "This is a great set. Chris Weitz is a genius. It is so wonderful." I was, "OK, dude, you are overselling." But I got on the set and it was just delightful. You can tell when it is uncomfortable and there is no connection. Chris Weitz is just a Zen master. I went to him and I was, "You are so cool and calm. And everyone is so cool and calm." He said, "You have no idea what it is going to cost me."

'My husband is a director and I know what it costs him. You have to tamp down every ounce of panic and frustration in order to project this calmness. I hope Chris got a good vacation between production and post-production.'

With the third and fourth movies (*Eclipse* and *Breaking Dawn*) in the works, it's clear that Robert is going to be associated with the character of the brooding vampire Edward Cullen for some time to come. But Robert is not someone to rest on his laurels and will be looking out for quirky roles to dispel any worries about typecasting. And the films that he has lined up should certainly quell those fears.

chapter thirteen

Future Roles

'It's one of the most lyrical scripts that I have ever read in my life.'
– Robert Pattinson

While Robert was delighted to be returning to the *Twilight* series, the commitment also meant missing out on a film he was desperate to star in. He had to turn down a role in *Parts Per Billion*. He had been delighted to take on the movie, as he told *Vanity Fair* about his future plans. 'I don't want to curse them, but I am doing this thing called *Parts Per Billion*, which is a kind of existential love story set against the end of the world. It stars three couples, three different generations. It's in LA. I have no idea how to explain it [but] it's one of the most lyrical scripts I have ever read in my life.'

Olivia Thirbly, who played Leah in *Juno*, was to star alongside Robert as one of the couples. She said of the plot, 'It's a beautiful, exquisite story about

three couples and it explores their relationships quietly. What's happening is there's a bio-terror attack happening as the film is unfolding and it's hard to explain what it's about.

'But at its core it's based on the idea that love is the most beautiful and the most prevailing life force and that ultimately it will carry us through to the other side. And it's a kind of quiet apocalypse that's happening and it's not front and centre of the film, but I don't know what else to say about it because I don't want to spoil the ending. It's one of the most beautiful scripts that I've ever read. It was written and is going to be directed by a fellow called Brian Horiuchi so keep an eye out. It's going to be really great.'

However, scheduling difficulties meant that Robert had to bail out of the film. 'Unfortunately, the prep time and production schedule on *New Moon* haven't left enough time for Robert to work on *Parts Per Billion* in the first quarter of this year,' confirmed his spokesperson.

But even before that statement, Rob had expressed concern that he was going to lose the part, because the start date of the smaller movie kept changing. 'That's the annoying thing about doing little things,' he lamented.

He did say, though, that while he was signing on for the *Twilight* sequels he was keen to ensure he kept doing other movies. 'I'm trying to fit in stuff between films,' he said. 'But it's nice at the same time

to actually be doing something which people care about, because then you can put effort into something. And even if people judge it badly, at least they'll be judging. At least they care about the outcome and they'll kind of analyse or whatever. So if you put enough work in hopefully it will pay off.'

Rob's first project outside the *Twilight* series is *Remember Me*, a drama that focuses on a relationship between Robert's Tyler Roth and Emilie de Ravin's Ally Craig as it bounces from happiness to tragedy. It's a film that he is hugely excited about, calling the script one 'where you finish and realise you didn't really want it to end.'

Summit, who made the *Twilight* films, snapped up Robert Pattinson – the jewel in their crown – for this movie as well. Announcing the film and their lead man to the press, they described the synopsis of the film like this: 'Pattinson plays a young man whose brother's suicide has split up his parents [Pierce Brosnan and Lena Olin] and left him sleepwalking through life. De Ravin will play a young woman who, after watching her mother get killed before her eyes, seizes life to its fullest. [Chris] Cooper is being courted to play her father.'

The media immediately seized on the pairing of Brosnan and Pattinson, seeing as Robert's name has been mentioned as a future James Bond. Wonder if Brosnan gave him any tips?

Robert said about the part, 'I read the script last

summer, and there was something about the character and way he spoke that was very similar to the way I speak. There is a naturalism to the writing and I really felt a connection to it. It's hard to describe. It's about a 23-year-old guy and knowing somebody for six weeks. You don't just fall in love and say "I'm in love" after six weeks. It's really a relationship story. It's very natural and the characters are incredibly real and well scripted.

'I have no qualms in saying that (the writer) Jenny Lumet is a genius. I went up to her one weekend and we all hung out and just chatted about the script and she asked me what I wanted from it. She worked on the draft and about a week later she delivered this script. She'd captured little bits of my voice and the mannerisms I have. The character in the script is quite similar to me.'

After that is the sweeping epic *Unbound Captives*. The film, written by actress Madeline Stowe, has been in the works for years. Hollywood has been desperate to put the story – about a young woman who seeks help from a frontiersman after her children are kidnapped by the Comanche tribe – on the big screen for years, but Stowe refused to sell it to the studios unless she played the lead role. She finally agreed to make the film after signing on to direct it instead. Rachel Weisz will now play the female part, with Robert teaming up along Hugh Jackman. It will mark Stowe's directorial debut.

Stowe actually cast Robert long before he hit it big with *Twilight*, so if her directing eye is half as good as her casting one then there should be no worries.

Robert's character, Phineas, has been described as a fierce, silent and standoffish warrior. Speaking about the part, Rob said, 'I can't say much about that, but I know the script needs me to learn Comanche. Maybe it'll be like *Dances with Wolves* with my part entirely in Comanche.'

The role is expected to see Robert flex his action muscles by getting into fights and riding horses bareback. However, *Anonymous.com* reports that he won't be appearing in the script until the latter stages of the movie. 'It is definitely a supporting role,' reports the site.

Robert has also signed on to star in 2011's *Bel Ami*, which is based on an 1885 short story. It sounds like we'll see Robert in a completely different light in this one. He plays a 'totally amoral' social climber, who manipulates a series of powerful and wealthy women to get what he wants.

As each film is different from each other, they will hopefully showcase Robert's diverse acting range. Meanwhile, *Twilight* fans will still get their fix. The fourth film is scheduled for 2011, but as there are rumours that they might be making a fifth, we could be seeing much more of Edward Cullen on the big screen yet.

chapter fourteen

Fame, Fans and Fangs

'The only thing I want from anything is to not be embarrassed.'
– Robert Pattinson

Fittingly for a self-confessed loner, Robert likes nothing better than just playing his piano and reading lots of books in his spare time – whatever spare time he gets now! 'I don't like relaxing too much – I feel like I'm wasting time,' he explains.

When Rob does socialise, it's with a small circle of loyal friends, old art students or new musician pals. 'Weirdly, I have the same group of friends as I had when I was in art school, but we've all, I guess, gone into our different fields and are very, very competitive with each other in relative subjects. My few best friends are all involved in music or art or writing. All of us seem to be coming up. I've always treated them really as pacemakers.

'The only people I try to please or try to impress

are my little group of friends. I don't really care about that much of a wider audience. I've thought that since I was 15 or 17.'

Despite his intense attitude at certain times, Rob does have a mischievous side. One lighthearted pastime involves making up names when he checks in at hotels. 'I was Clive Handjob in Paris. Everyone in the hotel called me Monsieur Handjob. That was good, cheap fun.'

He also entertains himself during interviews by making things up – a journalist's nightmare. '[I tell them] I do really intellectually highbrow stuff in my downtime. Like "I read first-edition Shakespeare books. I write poetry. I'm trying to get my masters in neuroscience. That's the kind of guy I am." Man, I don't even know what a masters is!'

One of the more persistent rumours about Robert that has followed him around, particularly in the US press, is that he has a drinking problem. There have been scores of eyewitness reports of Robert stumbling out of nightclubs the worse for wear, prompting speculation that he is struggling to cope with the huge media attention on him.

Hitting back at these claims, Robert explained, 'There isn't really like a pub thing in LA – it's just a very different culture. I think people from LA don't really understand how it's such a normal thing to be in pubs from a very young age in London. People just think it's so strange. Drinking has such a stigma

attached to it here. I have never really understood it. It seems so normal to me.

'In England, if you want to look rough you go out and get really drunk and come in looking really hung over, but if you do that in America it's like, "Have you got a drinking problem?"

'I keep getting photographed coming out of these lame clubs. It's so embarrassing. There was a week where every single night I was going out and getting photographed by the paparazzi or TMZ and I realised, "Oh my God, I look like a complete alcoholic."'

It was just an inkling that the media attention was beginning to take its toll on Robert, who was now beginning to realise that he couldn't even go out to a club without the media endlessly speculating about it.

He finally hit out during an interview with the *Guardian*, after he was asked about a comment he made where he seemingly dismissed the low-budget *Little Ashes* as 'nothing'.

'I hate having to do all this s**t!' he blasted. 'I've already been told to apologise for saying it. I was just trying to say that it was a tiny, little film. It had a miniscule budget. I was just trying to say that if *Twilight* hadn't come along I don't know how much *Little Ashes* would have been publicised. In an ideal world, everyone would go around watching art house films about Dalí and Lorca. But a lot of people have no idea who Lorca even was.

'People love all the negative stuff – "He doesn't even like the film". "He's a homophobe!" Oh, great.'

It all came about because of a quote to GQ magazine, in which he had said, 'It's nothing. It would never have been released. I mean, that's a terrible thing to say, but this was a movie where we didn't even have stand-ins! We were scrambling, the entire time. We didn't even have trailers.'

In a bid to appease the critics he even did something he hardly does – he watched his own performance in *Little Ashes*. 'It's like self-flagellation, so why would I bother? And I didn't want to piss on anyone's grave. It was hard to watch my first scene, in which I turn up in this funny little hat ... I was worried about watching them, but Dalí and Lorca's sex scenes were in fact the best scenes.'

The decision to watch the film comes as a sign that Robert is 'playing the game' more now than he used to. He still has his idealistic values, but he realises that there are additional pleasures that come with being a star. But Robert insists that there are some things that will never change. He will never desert his loyal group of friends, no matter how crazy it all gets.

'I don't feel like I've changed. The most embarrassing thing is when friends ask you to meet up with them and you have to tell them, "Sorry, I can't go to that place" because you're fully aware photographers will be waiting for you there.'

In another revealing quote about premieres, he

said, 'When I go, I guess I'm trying to promote it, but I'm not even promoting it. I'm just there to get screamed at. I don't even know what I'm supposed to be doing. The only thing I've done all year was go around cities and have people scream at me and stuff and ask things, like, "What's like to play the most beautiful person in the world?" It's surreal.

'I'm going to go back and start talking to my friends, being like, "Yeah, well this other person asked me how is it to play the most beautiful person in the world and then I went to this room and there's five thousand people screaming at me." I feel like I have nothing to talk about to my friends any more. It's going to destroy me when I go back home.'

Despite his fears, the future is bright for Robert. The media maelstrom surrounding him will inevitably fade away when a new Hollywood heartthrob takes his place, but unlike other actors who can get carried away by the hype, Robert is aware of how fickle the entertainment business can be. That's why he is focused on having a great body of work that stands the test of time, rather than just signing on to any script that comes his way.

'I prefer to do nothing than something stupid. I feel there's too much pressure because of this idea of 'career'. It's a little worrying. *Twilight* made so much money that now you're judged not by how good the film is, but by how much money the film you're in is making. That's the really scary thing now.'

Luckily for Robert, he has an actor in mind whose work pattern he would like to emulate. 'When you see a Jack Nicholson movie on DVD, you're pretty much guaranteed that there'll be something in it that is worth watching. That is, I think, the ideal thing to strive for. There are very few other actors where you can actually pick up any of their movies like that. Meryl Streep – pretty much all her movies are the same thing. I think that Leonardo DiCaprio is another, as well. I think that's why he kind of inspires me, just for that reason.'

But Robert is a free spirit, so whether it's acting, making music or finishing that novel he's long been writing, the one thing that's clear is that it will be a success because it's done on his terms.

'I'm not massively concerned about doing lots of acting. If it all just went right now I'd be like "All right, I don't really care." That's probably a stupid thing to say, but I don't, really. I think it'd be much worse to do a load of stuff that's really bad. Because then you can't go into another career. If you've made an idiot out of yourself, you're never going to be taken seriously, as a lawyer or something if you're, like, a joke actor. The only thing I want from anything is to not be embarrassed.'

And he certainly hasn't done that so far in his sometimes crazy, sometimes quiet but always interesting life.